# Literary Theory
## A Beginner's Guide

Clare Connors

ONEWORLD

OXFORD

A Oneworld Paperback Original

Published by Oneworld Publications 2010

Copyright © Clare Connors 2010

ISBN 978–1–85168–730–5

Typeset by Jayvee, Trivandrum, India
Cover design by Simon McFadden
Printed and bound by CPI Cox & Wyman, Reading, RG1 8EX

Oneworld Publications
UK: 185 Banbury Road, Oxford, OX2 7AR, England
USA: 38 Greene Street, 4th Floor, New York, NY 10013, USA
www.oneworld-publications.com

Learn more about Oneworld. Join our mailing list to find out about our latest titles and special offers at:

www.oneworld-publications.com

# Literary Theory
## A Beginner's Guide

**ONEWORLD BEGINNER'S GUIDES** combine an original, inventive, and engaging approach with expert analysis on subjects ranging from art and history to religion and politics, and everything in between. Innovative and affordable, books in the series are perfect for anyone curious about the way the world works and the big ideas of our time.

Beginners
GUIDES

# Contents

# Acknowledgements

Multiple writers and readers have made this book possible. I'm more grateful than I can say to Betty Connors, who read the whole manuscript as a 'beginner' to literary theory, and who also tracked down stray references. Charlie Louth, Ruth Cruickshank, Sarah Wood, Lydia Rainford and Forbes Morlock read draft chapters generously, attentively and critically. Two excellent readers at Oneworld, Marsha Filion and Dawn Sackett, provided invaluable help and advice in improving and preparing the manuscript. From school onwards, a number of teachers have helped me to think about how to read, and shown me how important reading is: I'm particularly indebted to Esmé Sibley, Stephen Lycett, Robert Jellicoe, Julia Briggs and Robert Smith. And my students at Queen's, Merton, Hertford and St. Catherine's Colleges, and at the Oxford University Department for Continuing Education continue to remind me why literature and literary theory matter: this book is for them.

# 1
# Introducing literary theory

> All theory, my friend, is grey.
> Life's golden tree is green.
> Goethe, *Faust, Part 1* (1808)

So whispers the diabolically persuasive Mephistopheles to a young man just beginning his studies. These words express a very common view of 'theory'. Theory is arid and abstract. Its generalizations wash life's vivid and variegated colours to an undifferentiated grey. To be a theorist is to sit on the margins, thinking distantly and dispassionately about life but never getting stuck in, never living. This set of anti-theoretical prejudices emerges with particular ferocity when people begin to contemplate *literary* theory: theory seems so much the opposite of literature that the words 'literary theory' sound like a contradiction in terms. To theorize about literature will, we fear, leach away the engaging, various and particular liveliness we prize it for. But it needn't do this. And this *Beginner's Guide* is animated by the conviction that the best forms of theory don't.

As we'll come to see, Mephistopheles is wrong on two fronts. For a start, theory can itself be full of colour and interest, drama and feeling. And second, theory is not something we can simply oppose to 'life', as the sophisticated, satanic seducer does in his insidiously simple couplet. We'll see instead how theory is muddled up with life, literature and practice – all those things to which it is customarily and too-easily opposed – from the first, and how, conversely, theory itself turns out to have literary properties. Theory is vital then, in both senses of that word: full of life and essential *to* life, and to the life of literature. But to say all this is to suggest that theory is in fact a rather different beast from the one we suspiciously imagine. Let's look first at our most usual, everyday sense of what 'theory' is.

## Theory and the Enlightenment

A theory, at least as it is understood in the sciences, is a structure of ideas that explains the data under scrutiny, or, as the *Oxford English Dictionary* has it, a 'hypothesis that has been confirmed or established by observation or experiment, and is propounded or accepted as accounting for the known facts' (*OED* sense 4). We can note here that 'hypothesis' is singular and 'the facts' plural. The theory of gravity accounts as competently for the fall of a boulder as it does for that of a banana, just as the theory of evolution describes the development of all living things, both animal and vegetable. Theory in its most usual, scientific or philosophical, twentieth-century sense is able, then, to subdue a variety of data to a single hypothesis.

This understanding of theory can be situated historically. Most modern scholarship and the theorizing it performs has its origins in the Enlightenment, that period of thought and enquiry across Europe which, as its name suggests, sought to shed light on all that was obscure. Enlightenment thinkers include Thomas Paine, author of *The Age of Reason* (1794), the philosophers Voltaire, Immanuel Kant, Spinoza and John Locke, the scientist Robert Hooke, the encylopaedist Denis Diderot and Ekaterina Dashkova, a polymath who became, remarkably for an eighteenth-century woman, the director of the St Petersburg Academy of Arts and Sciences. These thinkers often propounded diametrically opposed ideas. What they shared, however, was a desire to rid thought, science, political theory and philosophy of their dependence upon customs, institutions and untested suppositions or superstitions, and to reflect rationally and clear-sightedly about the world and about thought itself. Shining the light of reason on all aspects of the world, they sought to come to a lucid understanding of all manner of phenomena – scientific, cultural and linguistic. Such an understanding, it was hoped, would ultimately provide a rational account of every aspect of the world's workings.

These developments in thought and scholarship have had a profound effect on all areas of human knowledge, invention and production up to the present day. Nevertheless, it is possible to question their success, and indeed the extent of their neutrality. Michel Foucault, a twentieth-century theorist of history and of knowledge, has argued, for example, that the Enlightenment emphasis on reason operates as a power (see Foucault 1980). He claims that to know something (such as the habits and activities of a nation's population) is to have power over it. There is, for Foucault, then, a dangerous Big Brother-ism at work in the Enlightenment project.

While these questions are too large to pursue further here, what we can and must ask is whether *literature* can be viewed in the clear, rational light that Enlightenment thinking demands. Can it be taken as a simple object for knowledge? Can its diverse 'data' can be subdued to a single, elegant theory which would account for all the known facts about it? In keeping with the whole spirit of this *Beginner's Guide*, we will read some literature in order to explore that question.

## Reading literature

I've chosen a passage which deals with the reading of literature itself. We'll spend a while with it, reading it in order to tease out

the variety of phenomena any theory of literature would have to
address, as well as the problems that literature and reading might
pose to our ordinary understanding of theory. The passage comes
from a novel called *The Little Girls* (1963), written by the Anglo-
Irish writer Elizabeth Bowen. Here one of the three 'little girls'
of the book's title, Clare, enters the house of her friend's mother:

> To disturb Mrs Piggott once she was *in* a novel was known to
> be more or less impossible [...]. She was as oblivious of all parts
> of her person as she was of herself. As for her surroundings, they
> were nowhere. Feverel Cottage, the sofa, the time of day not
> merely did not exist for Mrs Piggott, they did *not* exist. This
> gave Clare, as part of them, an annihilated feeling. She burned
> with envy of anything's having the power to make *this* happen.
> Oh, to be as destructive as a story! (Bowen 1999, 78)

Mrs Piggott is '*in* a novel'. That underlined preposition 'in'
implies that the act of reading itself is not a distanced contem-
plation, but rather an immersion. And the passage goes on to
imply, rather more radically, that Mrs Piggott isn't really 'in'
anything – that, in a sense, she does not exist at all. Her reading
is not primarily to do with an 'eye' looking at a page, nor is it
to do with an 'I'. Mrs Piggott is 'oblivious' of the world of
things, people and furniture in which she lives, because she is
oblivious of 'all parts of her person' and even of 'herself'. The
world of things doesn't exist in this moment, because there is no
Mrs Piggott there for them to exist *for*.

Reading, in this account, then, seems to be to do with the
obliteration of both a subjective viewer and an objective
world. Enlightenment thinkers strove to bring their own rational thoughts to bear on objects and phenomena in the world.
But Bowen here suggests that reading is both the aggressive or
exhilarating annihilation of the world, *and* the blissful loss of a
self which could stand back from the world in order to view it
or to think rationally about it.

I think we might make the grander claim that this is a good way of describing what *always* happens in reading. When we read we are 'out of ourselves', inhabiting another place and another's words. At the same time, we are taken over and occupied *by* those words, as they displace our own thoughts in our reading minds. As we read the last longing line of free indirect discourse from our quotation – 'oh to be as destructive as a story' – a voice speaks within us which is not our own. Whether we want to or not, we voice inwardly a desire which is both ours and not ours as we read. We might wonder, then, what chance there is that a theory of literature could ever stand back dispassionately from its own reading, and therefore from what it theorized *about*. Just as reading seems to impassion, involve and obliterate Mrs Piggott and the world in which she exists, so, we might argue, it does similar things for us. And so to suggest that we can view literature neutrally, as a knowing subject facing a literary object, is to ignore the fact that literature can only be viewed through reading it and becoming involved in it, and that that involvement might always change us.

On the other hand, to say all this is already to have done more than simply immerse ourselves in reading the passage. We have offered a reading *of* it, quoting words from it in order to suggest what it is telling us about the dynamics of reading. Other analytical approaches could also be taken. We could think about the class implications of this scene, for example, and analyse its depiction of a genteel middle-class cottage and its owner, who has the leisure to lie about reading. We could also place it in larger literary-historical contexts. The figure of the female reader is one with a long literary history – think of Lydia Languish in Sheridan's *The Rivals* (1775), Catherine Morland, avid consumer of Gothic novels in Austen's *Northanger Abbey* (1818), or Jane Eyre, reading in her window seat at the start of the novel which bears her name. We might want to consider how Mrs Piggott – who is doubly 'in a novel', both reading one *and* a character in one – participates in this tradition. This passage hints at other literary contexts too: the name 'Feverel Cottage' will remind novel readers of George Meredith's *The Ordeal of Richard Feverel* (1859), a tale of intergenerational conflicts and the psychology of sexual repression and jealousy. It would be interesting to see how far one might take up the allusion to Meredith, in an exploration of the intergenerational relationship here between Mrs Piggott and the little girl Clare, who is bursting with violent impulses, and envious of Mrs. Piggott's absorption in her reading.

In all these ways it does seem possible to stand outside our reading of the passage in order to know it and analyse it. And here is where some theoretical reflections would be necessary, in order to justify our approach. What kind of links is it proper to make between a text and its sociological or literary-historical context? Do those contexts fix a work in its place? Or can it tell us about them? These are questions we'll explore in chapters 2 and 4 of this *Guide*. What does Bowen's account of the pleasures and annihilating violence of reading *tell* us about pleasure, and about the psyche? And how to account for the extraordinary, visceral, intellectual, uneasy pleasures of reading Bowen's strange, often witty, and superbly intelligent writing? Questions about reading and pleasure will be addressed in chapter 5. How to analyse the gender politics of this scene between an older, female reader, who is '*in* a novel' and an envious, desirous 'little girl', who aspires to be like a story? The relationship between literature and gender will be the concern of chapter 6 of this book. Is it significant that the Anglo-Irish Bowen here represents a situation in which the complacent occupier of a cottage and of a novel causes the marginalized outsider Clare to feel annihilated, to burn with envy, to wish for power and the power to destroy? Might we make comparisons here with her earlier novel, *The Last September* (1928), which depicts complacent members of the Anglo-Irish gentry in a country house in

Cork, obliviously playing tennis and dancing, while all around them the Irish 'Troubles' brew? Questions of literature's implication in imperial contexts, where occupation and marginality, power and violence, are to the fore, will be asked in chapter 7. Perhaps you think that a reading of this passage in terms of imperialism is taking things too far. We could argue that Bowen did not mean it to be read in this way. But what does it mean to take our reading too far? How do we decide on the legitimate meanings or interpretations of a text? We'll look at questions about authorial intention and meaning in chapter 3.

Insofar as we *can* stand outside our reading of the passage and offer an account of it, then, theoretical reflections which test and analyse the basis on which we undertake our readings would seem to be possible. Indeed, in order to *justify* our readings, some clear, lucid theoretical account of what is admissable in reading in general is absolutely necessary. But there's a twist here. Our more analytical and dispassionate reading of the passage has elicited a rather strange fact – which is that Bowen's writing is itself offering a *theory* of reading. Clare/Bowen articulate the idea of a story as 'destructive': the passage explores and makes claims about the effects reading has on the self and the world. The passage could, then, be said already to be undertaking the kind of thinking we seek to bring to bear on it. Insofar as it is offering a theory of reading, it seems to be theorizing *itself*.

What starts to emerge from our readings and reflections here, then, is that it seems at once necessary for us to have a theory of literature, in order to justify and ground our readings, and yet impossible for that theory to have any fixed ground, absolutely and neutrally outside the literary dynamics it wants to account for. Literature seems to require an almost exorbitant breadth of dispassionate scholarly knowledge (of other literature, of history, of psychology and so on), and a tight, clear theoretical account of what reading demands and entails, even while it also elicits – just by needing to be read – a readerly involvement in, and abandonment to, someone else's words. Furthermore, those words can, potentially, themselves reflect on and theorize literature and reading, and alter our sense of the contexts and histories in which we might want simply to place them. There's a final twist too. To claim, as I've just done, that Bowen's writing has self-reflexive or self-theorizing qualities, is to situate my arguments in relationship to ideas of literature which emerge out of 'post-Romantic' and 'theoretical' contexts. This idea of literature has its own histories – which could be read, reflected upon and theorized.

Attempting to theorize literature seems to put us in a spin or spiral, in which theories are necessary, but never fully adequate, and never able to extricate themselves totally from what they want to theorize about. Literature, in short, seems to present the would-be theorist with impossible demands. 'Literary theory' names at once a necessity and an impossibility.

## This book

While this book is called a guide to *Literary Theory*, there is, in fact, no such thing as 'literary theory' in a general sense. The term 'theory' is a shorthand way of describing a series of stabs, speculations, hypotheses and intellectual forays, which seek to provide the best account they can of different aspects of the thing we call 'literature'. These forays venture out from particular contexts: contexts which are institutional, geographical, intellectual, political, literary and personal. Theories themselves can be read, analysed, contextualized – the intentions of theorists can be asked after, their hidden motivations or ideologies explored. Different theorists are in dialogue with one another, as well as with literature.

No presentation of literary theories, then, can be absolutely neutral. We could, for example, offer an account of theories which contextualized them very precisely in terms of their emergence from specific social and economic situations. But such an historicist reading of theory would, therefore, already be working with its own implicit theory of history.

Let me, then, make my own intentions as clear as possible. The aim of this *Beginner's Guide* is to involve you – and more importantly to show that we are all, as readers of literature, already involved – in the debates that form the discipline of 'literary theory'. In each chapter we'll pursue a backwards and forwards movement between readings of specific literary works and the writings of specific literary theorists. Only the misconception of literary theory as something purely and abstractly conceptual leads to the Mephistophelian view of it as grey and rebarbative. Literary theory is a *process* of readings and reflections rather than a fixed set of ideas which can be packaged up and given to you. The best way to understand something is to participate in it – and that is what this book conjures you to do.

In the chapters that follow we'll read a range of theoretical statements alongside and in relation to literature, moving back and forth between the two, judging and testing, clarifying arguments, but also noticing, reading and analysing how theoretical claims are *made*. In each chapter, I've taken a single, short, strange work of literature as the focus for my readings. They are: Gerard Manley Hopkins's 'As Kingfishers Catch Fire', Joseph Conrad's 'The Secret Sharer', Charles Dickens's *Hard Times*, Annie Proulx's *Brokeback Mountain*, Christina Rossetti's 'Goblin Market' and Rider Haggard's *She*. It's not necessary for you to have read these – in each case I give an account of what the text is about, as well as quoting amply from it. On the other hand, I should say that I've chosen these works because they are by turns inspiring, engaging, interesting, odd, brilliantly-written, funny and moving. And that my hope is that, if you haven't read them before you start this book, you'll want to by the time you've finished.

At this juncture you could stop reading this introduction, and cut straight to the first chapter. What I'm going to do in the second half is to give a brief survey of the whole terrain of 'literary theory', suggesting some of its broader features, and offering some, necessarily partial, accounts of the contexts from which it emerged. You might find these helpful as a way of orienting yourself before you plunge in. On the other hand, you might prefer to return to them later, once you have already engaged in some literary-theoretical reflections and readings.

# The histories of literary theory

Theoretical musings about literature – on what it is, how it works, on what it can and ought to do, how best to treat or read it, and what role it does or should play in our lives – have gone on for millennia. Literary theory may well be as old as literature itself, and we can certainly date it back to pre-Socratic thinkers. *The Norton Anthology of Theory and Criticism* (Leitch 2001) for example, a 2,625-page tome, begins with an excerpt from the work of Gorgias of Leontini, a writer of the fourth century BC, in which he discusses the power and function of speech and of rhetorical or poetical language. The anthology then moves through Plato and Aristotle, medieval and Renaissance theorists of rhetoric, eighteenth- and nineteenth-century philosophers, feminists and political theorists and twentieth-century linguists, psychoanalysts and cultural historians, to name but a few, concluding with the late twentieth-century work of Stuart Moulthrop, a theorist of cyber-text. Literary theory, as represented here, names a whole – Western – tradition of reflections on language, meaning and literature.

But in fact, neither Gorgias of Leontini nor most of the other people gathered together in the *Norton Anthology* – Mary Wollstonecraft, Sigmund Freud, Karl Marx and so on – would have thought they were carrying out 'literary theory'. They would have seen themselves as philosophers or rhetoricians, as linguists or political theorists, as scientists or psychoanalysts. What's more, the very idea of 'literature' as we use it today would not have been known to most of the people in this collection. Until the eighteenth century, 'literature' referred to any kind of reading matter, and people talking more precisely about what *we* call literature would have referred to poetry or drama, or more generally 'letters', which included things like biography and history as well as fictional writing.

While reflections on what we now call literature have a long tradition, the *term* literary theory, and often just plain 'theory' – along with the idea of *being* a theorist or *doing* theory – has a much shorter history than the ages spanned by the *Norton Anthology*. Several of the theorists we will go on to read later in this book have dated the naming of 'theory' as an identifiable field roughly to the 1960s. Paul de Man, for example, refers to the 'post-1960 sense of the term' (de Man 1986, 6), and Hélène Cixous says that 'since the 1960s this term has belonged to the lexicon of the intra-academic ideological war' (Cixous 1999, 211).

In fact, the main feature of 'theory' in this newfangled sense is precisely one which explains the broad temporal and disciplinary sweep of the *Norton Anthology*. Post-1960s theory, that is to say, is a form of thinking which greedily assimilates work from other disciplines and is hospitable to writing which isn't overtly about literature. As Jonathan Culler has observed, the post-60s theory corpus is defined by the very fact that it comprises 'works that succeed in challenging and reorienting thinking in fields other than those to which they ostensibly belong' (Culler 1987, 87). He points out that Freud and Nietzsche are today more often studied on 'theory' courses in literature departments than by students in the fields of psychology or philosophy. Modern literary theory, then, is a mobile, mongrel, magpie and upstart creature. It reaches back in time to claim past thinkers as its own, traverses disciplinary borders and shelters migrants and foreign bodies within its own domain. The *Norton Anthology* (and others like it such as Raman Selden's *The Theory of Criticism: From Plato to the Present* (Selden 1988) or Rivkin and Ryan's *Literary Theory: An Anthology* (Rivkin 2004)) represents and arises from this process. Such anthologies are a result of 'theory' in its 'post-1960s' sense. Theorists read literature and think and write helpfully about it by drawing on their own avid and wide-ranging reading of 'non-literary' writings: sociological, anthropological, scientific, linguistic, philosophical, political and so on. These writings in themselves can be studied as part of the corpus of literary theory.

Our reading of the quotation from Elizabeth Bowen suggested already why literary theory might exist as this hybrid and heterogeneous field. We have seen how a small excerpt from a single work of literature can touch on a whole range of domains, demanding that one reflect upon history and context, on gender, class and power, on meaning and intention, and on the nature of reading itself. And when we consider everything that goes by the name of literature, we can conclude that literature quite simply can be about *everything*. Literary theory would just *have* to be a wide-reaching, hybrid, polymorphous discipline, in order to grapple with the wide-reaching, hybrid and polymorphous object it wants to theorize *about*. What's more surprising, in fact, is that literary theory is such a recent phenomenon. It would seem that literature has always cried out for the kind of multi-disciplinary attention that it has apparently only received in the last half century. Why, then, is literary theory such a new thing? The answers to this question can tell us much about what literary theory is today.

# The study of literature: foreign bodies

The emergence of 'literary theory' as a field of speculative study is intimately linked to the history of the study of literature itself. And that history is a complex and compelling one – bound up with questions of power, resistance and freedom. The first thing to make clear is that the *study* of literature itself is a very new one. While, in Western Europe, Classical literature had been studied in universities since the Renaissance, literature in the *vernacular* – in the language actually spoken in the culture at large – did not become a subject for study until the nineteenth century (at which time it also entered the curricula of American universities). The interwoven factors which account for the emergence of vernacular literature as a suitable subject for academic study can helpfully be summed up by the single word 'democracy'.

The rise of literacy across the West went hand-in-hand with movements towards electoral and legislative reform, which in turn produced growing numbers of people – women, and members of the hitherto disenfranchised lower and middle classes – who were entitled and educationally equipped to attend university. In the United States, the first single-sex colleges were founded – alongside a few co-educational ones – in the early nineteenth century. British women had to wait until the foundation of Girton College, in Cambridge, in 1869, for an institution of their own. Women, and men from the less-privileged classes of society, gradually became free, then, to study at university. But in the main they did not have a background in Latin and Greek, a knowledge of which was essential to most humanities courses; and women were still debarred from entry into professions such as law and medicine. Vernacular literature had, however, for some time been studied in evening classes and working men's colleges in Britain and in women's seminaries in the United States. It was – as Terry Eagleton has put it – 'literally the poor man's Classics' (Eagleton 27). And so, slowly, as 'poor men' and women entered the university and their children entered the school room, so too did the study of vernacular literature. Vernacular literature thus became – from the mid-nineteenth century in both Britain and the States – what we think of as a 'proper' subject, available to be taught, studied and researched.

At the same time, and connected with these developments, writers and thinkers had started to reconsider the entitlements of literature *itself* – what it could and couldn't do, and what kind of subject matter might be admitted to its hallowed portals. For example, Wordsworth's 'Preface' to the collection of poems *The Lyrical Ballads*, which he first published with Coleridge in 1798, defends trenchantly his treatment of rural characters and the 'incidents of common life', on the grounds that in humble environments 'our elementary feelings exist in a state of greater simplicity and consequently may be more accurately contemplated and more forcefully communicated' (Wordsworth, 245).

While literature had – since before Chaucer – engaged with all manner of 'humble' subjects, Wordsworth's claims that these subjects offered the profoundest access to human truth and value were relatively new. In the nineteenth century, literature came to be seen as the place where the most important questions of human being could be discussed and where the value of the human itself could best find expression and be preserved. Such views about what literature is, and ought to be able to include, are themselves linked also to political movements and convictions; in particular to the revolutionary demands for the 'rights of man' which resounded throughout Europe from the late-eighteenth century well into the nineteenth, and the claims – initially more stifled but no less forceful – for the 'rights of woman'. Some authors were directly engaged in these movements. Wordsworth was a fervent supporter of the French

Revolution in its early stages, for example, while Byron was involved in the Greek war of independence against the Ottoman Empire. Such political developments were, in turn, connected with and animated by the Enlightenment project of shunning prejudice and the tyranny of fossilized institutional ideas, in favour of the clear, neutral light of human reason.

The democratic opening of the doors of academic institutions, which led to the study of vernacular literature chimed, then, with the opening up of literature to new voices and possibilities, which were, at least in principle, cherished in their own right. And both of these emancipatory openings were linked to broader movements towards equal rights and democracy, which aimed at the banishment of social orders based on class, gender, faith, ethnicity and calcified tradition.

It would not do to be too naively celebratory here, of course, and much less up-beat accounts of these developments are possible. Terry Eagleton suggests, for example, that the emergence of literary studies was driven by profound *ideological* imperatives, and that literature became a new way of inculcating moral values: an opiate for the masses. In a period in which age-old truths were being questioned, literature came to be seen as a new touchstone of universal truth, and a way of staving off the collapse of civilization which revolutionary movements threatened. It could always be invoked and employed in conservative interests then, and as a way of enforcing, in subtle ways, new rules and laws. We might also point here to the way that the teaching of English and French literature in the colonies, at the expense of indigenous African and Indian literatures, was deeply complicit with the oppressive and racist agendas of imperialism and colonialism – a subject I'll return to in chapter 7 of this book.

But while these arguments are not without their truth, what I want to underscore here are the possibilities and institutional anxieties which the developments I've outlined simultaneously opened up. Works of literature, increasingly understood as places where *everyone's* voices may be heard and where *everything* in principle might be said, became the object of scholarly study, at the same time as universities, colleges and schools opened their doors to people who would hitherto have been cleaning their chimneys or confined to the home, factory or field. The foundation of literature as an academic discipline is doubly linked, then, with the introduction of new and foreign bodies into venerable institutional and intellectual scholarly traditions.

Literature, then, has a rather odd relationship to the institution in which it comes to be studied. The thinker of deconstruction, Jacques Derrida, has called literature a 'strange institution which allows one to say everything' (Derrida 1992: 37). Literature is an institution in two ways. First, it is always instituted by things outside it – for example by the contexts in which it is written, which define what literature *is*. We can see that in the Romantic redefinition of literature in Wordsworth's writing, and Eagleton's forceful reading of such redefinitions. Cultures, contexts, ideological forces and academic institutions institute particular views of what literature is. But second, literature itself institutes – installing, between the pages of a book, the very rules and structures which make the worlds it conjures up meaningful to us as we read. And by doing so it always allows us to reflect on worlds, institutions and rules themselves. Literature is not some free-floating entity – it is dated and signed, marked by the time and place from which an individual writes it. But because it can always reflect on that time and place, it can always speak back to it, and open up some leeway for new possibilities within the institutions in which it is read and studied.

# The discipline of literary criticism

What the introduction of vernacular literature into the university leads to is a rather dramatic situation. After all, once something becomes teachable in academic institutions it forms a discipline. As such, it must be taught and examined, and protocols and standards for doing this must be agreed on. Literary study would be impossible to defend *as* a discipline, worthy of academic accreditation and also – increasingly crucially – of *funding*, if it could not be measured, taught and tested. But how to make teachable and testable this amorphous, rich, various thing called literature, with its polyphony of voices, its capacity to talk about anything, and its involvement, therefore, in every other discipline there is? It seems impossible to take literature as the focus of one discipline amongst others – to *discipline it*. Literature's involvement in everything – and its capacity also to talk about itself, and its own involvement in everything – makes it untameable by the usual disciplinary protocols.

Institutions seeking to promote research into and teaching of literature are therefore in a bind. On the one hand, they want to cherish literature and be true to it. Scholarship is built on its fidelity to and pursuit of truth, and this, quite rightly, hasn't changed since the Enlightenment. But to make something the object of scholarship is to make it knowable, teachable and testable. And the kind of fidelity literature demands seems to ruin all the well-tried academic methods for producing and arriving at truth. The deconstructive and eco-theorist Timothy Clark has called this the tension between 'literary force and institutional values' (Clark 2002). It's a bind that we still inhabit today, and we'll see it played out repeatedly and always-differently across the pages of this *Beginner's Guide*. Any attempt simply to legislate about literature is doomed to failure. But in order to read literature faithfully we need to have some rules to determine what a faithful reading would be. How to preserve and defend literature as valuable and worthy of study and funding, without subjecting it to rules and measurements which take away what is most precious about it? Literary theory has its origins in this dilemma.

## The origins of theory

The first moves to defend and justify the study and teaching of literature in clear, generalizable terms came in the early decades of the twentieth century. And the form they took bears the marks of the institutional predicament from which they emerged. They represented attempts to define what was specific and unique to literature *as such*. We can see how this would be necessary. If literature is, as we have said, a 'strange institution which allows one to say everything', and which can incorporate all other disciplinary domains within its own sphere, it is at once incredibly powerful but also very weak. If literature can be anything, then it can always be claimed that it is nothing special. I think we probably all find this as readers or students of literature – it can be hard to justify what we do. It doesn't seem very 'proper'.

Attempts to define what was 'proper' to literature occurred in various parts of the world almost simultaneously. In Russia, in the 1920s, they happened within the literary and linguistic movement which is now called 'Russian Formalism', which we'll discuss more in the next chapter. In Britain they are linked to the names of F. R. Leavis and I. A. Richards. The former, in the literary criticism he published in books and in his journal *Scrutiny*, offered a series of trenchant defences of literature's morally nourishing and enriching qualities, and its capacity to tell us about 'life'. The latter inaugurated the practice sometimes known as 'practical criticism', in which a text – usually a poem – is read without reference to its author or its context. Richards's first aim was not, in fact, to formulate a theory of what literature was. 'Practical criticism' arose from a series of forensic investigations into how people actually read, in which he gave undergraduate students in Cambridge unattributed poems to read, and analysed the 'errors' of interpretation they made, when they had no other points of anchorage to ground their readings. These experiments – published in a book called *Practical Criticism* (1930) – inspired and influenced a group of critics writing in the United States, who became known as the New Critics. They took Richards's experiment as providing a model for how reading should ideally operate – focusing solely on 'the words on the page'.

We'll discuss all these approaches further in the next chapter, for they are essential to the question 'what is literature?'. But they are also – in their nuanced and serious insights into literature, as well as in their flaws and shortcomings – essential to the very emergence of literary theory. What they all suggest, in different ways, is that literature, while it can be about absolutely anything, *does* things that no other kind of writing does. Literature, in this account, represents particular ways of doing things with words. For Russian Formalists, literature makes language strange to us in ways that prompt us to see the world anew. And for Practical and New Critics, it represents particularly compact, perfectly formed, artfully constructed, patternings and arrangements of words and meanings, which make of the literary work an exquisite and nuanced complex of sound and sense. In order to elicit the unique qualities of works of literature, particular, disciplined critical techniques are thus required. These English and American critics inaugurate the practice known as close reading, which we'll be enacting and discussing explicitly in chapter 2 and which informs many of the readings (of literature *and* of theory) throughout this book. These critics look closely at literary works – usually poems – with a respectful and interested gaze, scrutinizing their *verbal* as well as their physical structures, paying attention, as they say, to 'the words on the page' and exploring the way in which a text's elements and parts – its symbols, rhythms, rhymes, the particular choice of a word, and any potential ambiguities of meaning – are disposed and juxtaposed. Moving sensitively back and forth between discussions of elements of a work and its overall meaning, which emerges with greater richness and precision as the process advances, they show how everything in it fits together, efficiently, convincingly and pleasingly. The aim of literary criticism is, as the New Critic W. K. Wimsatt has put it, 'to give a valid account of the relation between poetic form and poetic meaning' (1965, 244). And the essence of literature as an object of study exists precisely in this 'relation'.

Leaving aside here the question of how adequate this definition of literature is – the business of the next chapter – we can point out one crucial thing about it, which is that *as* a definition, however modest and delicately phrased, it throws down a gauntlet. That is to say that, in so far as these early twentieth-century literary critics do offer definitions of literature, these can always be tested and challenged. Once we are offered a 'theory' about literature – which is 'propounded or accepted as accounting for the known facts', to requote our dictionary definition of theory – we are, at least in principle, always free to appeal to other literary 'facts' to contest it. What does it leave out? Does all literature fit this bill? What hidden assumptions are implicit within this definition? Might it not apply to things that *aren't* literature too? By seeking to define carefully and precisely what literature is, in order to justify the study of literature as an independent discipline and a valuable pursuit, Russian Formalists, Practical Critics, and New Critics such as W. K. Wimsatt can be said to have issued a challenge. And the challenge they pose is in great part responsible for inaugurating all the subsequent ripostes, arguments and discussions that go under the name of 'literary theory' in its 'post-1960s' sense. These debates will be traced in detail throughout this *Beginner's Guide*. What I'll do in the last section of this introduction is to look, very briefly, at some of the positions and places from which they emerge.

## Literary theory post-1960s

Any attempt to engage with, to study or to teach literature must privilege some literary texts over others. This is not in principle a question of hidden agendas: there is simply not enough time to read or study all the literature there is in the world. But this general and agonizing situation, the predicament of being mortal human beings, leads to institutional, political and ethical implications. Choices have to be made. And the *reasons* behind those choices can therefore always be scrutinized. In the case of the Practical and the New Critics, we might ask, for example, why they mainly focus on – relatively short – poems in their literary analyses. Is it because these are easier to view as organic wholes than novels or plays for example? Might it be because they are easier to teach within a seminar context? Or cheaper to teach, in institutional contexts where student numbers are increasing but resources are finite?

In the 1950s and 1960s, in the context of feminist, socialist, civil rights and protest movements in Europe and the United States, other questions about the reasons for the choices behind curricula and syllabi were also posed. Why did the literature taught in schools and universities, and valued in the culture at large, tend to be by white, middle-class men? If literature can – in principle – say anything, then why did the literature chosen for study seem only to talk about a limited sphere of human existence, and to be written by only a small portion of humankind? These questions, while they were asked with justifiable force, did not challenge either the value of literature, or, necessarily, the idea that a close reading of it was important. What they did suggest was that the treatment and definition of literature as the relation between form and meaning still relied on a more general assumption that we knew what literature was: that we could reach for the examples that would demonstrate literariness and bear analytical fruit. These assumptions meant that the discipline of literary study was itself still shot through with pre-suppositions that weren't purely literary.

On the other hand, socialist, feminist and civil rights activists also wondered whether literature could *ever* be purely literary.

How are literature's forms and meanings bound up with the forms and meanings we find in the world at large? More particularly, how might it be caught up in promulgating particular ideas of gender, of class or of ethnicity? Or, conversely, can it help us think about these things differently? These are some of the questions we'll discuss in chapters 4, 6 and 7 of this book.

Other intellectual movements and strains of thought also challenged some of the New Critical assumptions about literature. If language and literature are powerful forces in the world, then attention must be paid to what language *is*. And radical theories about the nature and workings of language were, at the start of the twentieth century, being propounded by the Swiss theorist Ferdinand de Saussure, and as the century proceeded, taken up by scholars in the whole area of the humanities – in anthropology, sociology, classics and philosophy for example. What Saussure suggested, in brief, was that *all* meaning, within a particular language at a specific moment, could be understood in terms of structured networks, comprising what he calls signs. Signs are made up on the one hand of a signifier – the part of the sign that we see and hear – and on the other the signified, the concept which the signifier calls to mind. For Saussure, within any single language, the network of different signifiers are locked together with the network of different signifieds, by the implicit set of rules that we subscribe to when we speak a particular language. Meaning is a result of structures.

Saussure revolutionizes our idea of language. And he imagines his own modest and local account of differences within languages as a small part of a larger project. He writes that it 'is possible to conceive of a science which *studies the role of signs as part of social life*' (Saussure 1983, 15). This prompt was taken up in the 1950s and 1960s by a number of theorists and critics known as structuralists and semiologists, who applied Saussure's ideas about *linguistic structure* to all meaningful human things in the world. They suggested that we might read adverts, courtship rituals, myths, novels and poems as structures in which any one element makes sense because of its place within a larger structure, which has no inherent meaning itself, but is held in place because we silently agree to its terms.

We'll explore the details and question the merits of the structuralist approach in chapter 3, when we look in detail at the question of literary meaning. For now, we can say certain things about it as a *phenomenon* within the emergence of literary theory. Structuralism represents a powerful theoretical tool, which could accord the study of literature a more rigorous and precise quality than it had hitherto had. It also demonstrates how literature is bound up with other meanings and relationships in the world – with larger structures and organizing patterns. But on the other hand, it removes from literature any intrinsic value or properties of its own. The interplay between form and meaning which New Critics see as essential and unique to *literature*, is taken up as a more general description of how any meaning at all is produced. Anything readable or interpretable can in principle be addressed in terms of the structures which govern and enable its meanings. Literature becomes, once again, indefensible as a subject for study 'in its own right'. It is merely one example amongst others of a structure.

Structuralism did not last long as a theoretical movement. It quickly became apparent that, as a way of approaching *any* kind of meaning, it missed too much out. For a start, and as Jacques Derrida has said, it reduced anything that didn't fit into the structural model it identified, to 'the inconsequentiality of accident or dross' (Derrida 2001, 29). It reduced local greens and golds to an indifferent grey. Attempting to find governing structures, it high-handedly ignored anything that didn't fit into them. And it therefore also ignored its own *role* in the process of reading. Related to this, it covered over the fact that reading *is* a process. Structuralism ignored the way in which literature unfolds over time, delays, throws us off course, echoes and quotes, places emphasis on some things and not on others – on the way it moves, and moves its reader.

On the other hand, structuralism itself disclosed future possibilities and ways of thinking about literature. In particular the idea that meaning was produced through *differences* and *relationships,* opened up ways of thinking about the process of reading as something dynamic – as an encounter in which one meaning supplants, refines or extends another, and in which literature is a force-field of meanings. We'll explore many of the directions in which this idea might take us throughout this *Beginner's Guide*.

A rethinking of how meaning works does not solely arise from the writings of Saussure and the work of the structuralists, however. We can also trace it back to intellectual adventures in philosophy undertaken in Germany from the start of the twentieth century. The German philosopher Edmund Husserl, inaugurator of an approach to knowledge called phenomenology, elaborated a way of thinking which aimed at capturing and articulating *how* we know the world. Rather than attempting, as earlier epistemologists such as Descartes had done, to ground and prove the objective existence of the world and therefore secure a knowledge of it, Husserl sought to describe the shape of the knowing self's relation to phenomena as they appear *to* it. His approach 'bracketed' the objective existence of the world, in favour of an attention to the mode of its appearance to the 'I'. This approach was taken up as a resource for the reading of literature by theorists including Stanley Fish and Wolfgang Iser (whose writings we'll explore in chapters 2 and 3, respectively). Their approach to reading literature became known as 'reception' or 'reader-response' theory. They suggested that we should explore literary works not for their objective structures, or for the intentions conveyed by their authors, but in terms of how they disclose themselves *to us*.

But, from the nineteenth century and across the twentieth century, the *nature* of 'us' – as human beings and as readers – was also being discussed, analysed and redescribed. The writings of Marx – which we'll explore in chapter 4 – put the 'us' back into accounts of human subjectivity. He imagines human beings not as originally separate individuals, but as always emerging from contexts of involvement with others – involvement that arises initially from our implication as social beings in a world in which resources must be shared. Marx's theories of 'alienation' and of 'ideology' describe the ways in which – unbeknownst to us – the originally social nature of our being is repressed and covered over. 'Ideology', as an ever-shifting and repeatedly refined concept, offers for many readers of literature – including feminists and post-colonial critics as well as those working explicitly in a Marxist tradition – a powerful way of thinking about the fictions always at work in our world. It can help us explore the stories that culture promotes in order to dissimulate the injustices which arise from unequal distribution of resources that ought in principle to be available to all. And it can also prompt us to think about how *literary* stories might participate in, or reflect upon, these cultural stories.

If Marx describes one kind of unknowingness, Freud's theories about the unconscious articulate another. We'll discuss it in detail in chapter 5. Freud's account of the psyche as a field of conflicting forces and desires, in which some must be repressed in order for us to survive in the world, leads to an understanding of much human communication happening in oblique or symbolic ways. Dreams, for Freud are 'disguised fulfilments of a suppressed wish' (Freud, 4, 160) – and more generally many of our articulations disguise, unbeknownst to us, wishes which can only be expressed in a shifty and covert form.

Marx's theory of ideology, and Freud's of the unconscious, point to well-springs of fiction-making power within the world at large. Oblique or symbolic expressions, and dissimulated meanings and truths, are no longer simply the province of literature. But neither are they innocent of a relationship to the world. These theories led to a series of reconsiderations of the relationship *between* literature and these ostensibly non-literary fictions and fabrications, in the work of psychoanalytic and political theorists of literature, in feminist and queer theorists, theorists who think about the ideologies at work in colonialism and imperialism and in all readers and theorists who attempt to account, in whatever way, for a text's meanings.

I could continue. But it's not my intention to offer an exhaustive history of the origins of literary theory here. I hope, rather, to have sketched out some of the ways in which – once literature becomes a focus of academic study, and attempts are made to justify it as such – its nature, workings and effects become a matter of discussion and often disagreement. And to have shown that these disagreements can open up new possibilities for reading, and disclose new aspects of literature itself.

It's to those possibilities that we will now turn. I hope you will find them as exciting, as stimulating, as fruitfully difficult, as occasionally absurd or irritating, and as potentially downright life-changing, as I do. There's no guarantee that you will. I cannot determine how you will read this book, or how you will read the literature and theories it discusses and quotes. My writing is entrusted to you, relies upon your engagement and risks – but perhaps also needs – your disagreement. Like the manuscript in the box that 'the little girls' bury in Elizabeth Bowen's wonderful novel, written in an 'Unknown language' and bequeathed to future unknown generations, this book depends on you, my unknown reader, reading it too. It is entrusted to 'chance, and its agents time and place' just as, as Clare thinks at the end of *The Little Girls,* we are 'entrusted to one another' (236). Let us, then, take our chances.

# 2
# What is literature?

This question is a strange one. On the one hand, it's a fundamental, first-order question. It asks about the nature of what it is that, as students and lovers of literature, we read. It requires us to define our terms and agree on our field and object of study. On the other hand 'what is literature?' is by no means the first question any reader of literature ever asks themselves. It's a late-coming question – and therefore a question that demands that we reflect *back* on our own reading, looking on it with new eyes.

It can be helpful to do this. Asking what literature is enables us to lay bare the implicit assumptions that we operate with as we read it. If we *don't* reflect on these assumptions they might well skew our thinking and prejudice our writing in unhelpful ways. So, for example, if we say that we prefer Elizabeth Gaskell's *North and South* (1855) to Dickens's *Hard Times* (1854) because it is more realistic, then we are implicitly assuming that what we expect of literature, or at least of the novel, is a faithful rendition of life: that literature, for us, is its best self, most *literary*, when it mirrors the world rather than, for example, caricaturing it, or fantasizing about it or inventing new possibilities for it. If we reflect more on the question of what literature *is*, then we might, at the very least, have better reasons to justify our judgements, or indeed, want to revise those judgements. New literary possibilities might also be opened up for us in the process.

Many theorists over the years have asked the question 'what is literature?'. In the course of this chapter we will explore some of their arguments, focusing in particular on the work of New

Critics, Russian Formalists, reader-response theorists and theorists working with deconstruction. But because we all start here – I imagine – from the position of being readers and lovers of literature, I want to begin with a particular piece of literature – Gerard Manley Hopkins's 'As kingfishers catch fire' (1877). No point of departure is neutral: this is already a loaded decision. When literary theorists make general claims about what literature is, they are always open to questioning about their choice of examples. In this case, you might quite rightly object that my choice risks suggesting that the best or truest literature is poetic. This is a question we'll bear in mind as we proceed.

My (conscious) reasons for beginning here are two fold, and at once deeply personal, and respectably academic. First, I've chosen this sonnet because my Dad first taught me to love it, and I now think it's an amazing piece of literature – whatever that means. But second, it's a poem that is actually engaged in asking the question *what is*. It's not in the first instance asking 'what is literature?' but it is asking about the essence of things, about 'whatness'. We can use the poem's own thinking about the question of *what something is* to help us to think about 'what literature is'.

## A poem

'As kingfishers catch fire'
As kingfishers catch fire, dragonflies draw flame;
　As tumbled over rim in roundy wells
　Stones ring; like each tucked string tells, each hung bell's
Bow swung finds tongue to fling out broad its name;
Each mortal thing does one thing and the same:
　Deals out that being indoors each one dwells;
　Selves – goes its self; *myself* it speaks and spells,
Crying What I do is me: for that I came.

I say more: the just man justices;
  Keeps grace: that keeps all his goings graces;
Acts in God's eye what in God's eye he is –
  Christ. For Christ plays in ten thousand places,
Lovely in limbs, and lovely in eyes not his
To the Father through the features of men's faces.

You'll probably find that you want to read this poem aloud to yourself once or twice to get the feel of it. Most people's immediate reaction to it – and to Hopkins's poetry in general – is to balk at its strangeness. On the other hand, before we even get to its sense, we can enjoy its euphony, its feel in the mouth and on the tongue, its chimes and rhymes and rhythms, the way *it* rings and tells and speaks and spells. A pleasure in sound and the sensual aspects of language forms no small part of what literature gives us. And often when we try to define what is special about literature, it is its cultivation of the pleasurable, material, rhythmic, rhetorical and ornamental aspects of language that we think of. Before we even begin to analyse the poem, then, we might wonder whether our initial response to it has disclosed to us the essence of literature. *Is* literature a particularly fancy way of using language?

## Figurative language

Throughout the ages, literary language has been associated with its use of ornaments and figures. This understanding of literariness does not belong to a particular theoretical 'school', but it is nevertheless there in many discussions of literary language, and so needs to be addressed. Here's the sixteenth-century rhetorician George Puttenham on the subject of figurative language and its relationship to literature:

As figures be the instruments of ornament in every language, so be they also in a sorte abuses or rather trespasses in speach,

because they passe the ordinary limits of common utterance [...]
but in this case, because our maker or Poet is appointed not for
a judge, but rather for a pleader, and that of pleasant & lovely
causes and nothing perillous [...] all his abuses tende but to
dispose the hearers to mirth and sollace by pleasant conveyance
and efficacy of speach, they are not in truth to be accompted
vices but for vertues in the poetical science very commendable.
(Puttenham 1968, 128)

Puttenham distinguishes here between the 'common utterance'
appropriate for everyday transactions or the neutral language of
the courtroom, and the gently persuasive language of art, where
ornaments need not be regarded as suspicious but rather are its
virtue. He expresses a very common view and one we might still
hold. He implies that fancy, ornate, overtly stylish or figurative
language is a defining property of literary writing. But does literature's *essence* lie in its use of rhetorical figures, and its deployment of an ornamented, fancy, high style?

Take an excerpt such as this:

The DES, through the UGC, have urged the CVCP to ensure
that universities throughout the UK [...] make a special effort in
the coming year to show themselves responsive to the needs of
industry, both in terms of collaboration in research and development, and the provision of well-trained and well-motivated
graduates for recruitment to industry.

Is it literary or not? There's a marked absence of rhetorical
figures – no nice metaphors here, no juicy alliteration, no
rhyme, no distinctive rhythm. It's depressingly similar, both in
its language and its thinking, to the bureau-speak that has infil-
trated all levels of education over the last three decades and
which demands that teaching – including the teaching of literature – have a measurable and immediate utility. There's none of
the rather disconcerting flaunting of language's possibilities that

we see in Hopkins's sonnet. But this is, nevertheless, from a work of literature: David Lodge's *Nice Work* (1988, 84–5), a satire on the Thatcher government's narrowly-interested politicization of university teaching in Britain in the 1980s, and a meditation on what literature is and can do. We could find many sentences, in many novels and plays, and poems too, (think of Larkin's 'they fuck you up, your mum and dad' in his poem 'This Be The Verse' (1971)), which do not bespeak an overt literariness, do not, that is to say, exploit the resources of rhetoric, figuration, rhyme and rhythm.

*Conversely*, we can find many instances of figural or alliterative or rhythmic or rhyming language in non-literary forms. Look, for example, at the tongue-twister I wrote for a friend: 'imperturbable baby babbled 'n' burbled impressively impervious to the improbability of the probabiliorists' propaganda'. Think too of advertising slogans – such as 'see the USA in a Chevrolet' or 'Guinness is good for you'. Or what about the following sentence – 'All I know is that to see, and not to speak, would be the great betrayal'? In 'blind literature tastings' my students invariably identify this as 'literary'. And it is easy to see why. It has a gravity and measured poise not found in 'common utterance' and its sentiment – that it is treacherous to see an injustice and not to speak out against it – is inspiring. But the sentence in fact comes from the odious and racist 'rivers of blood' speech, given by the English far-right-wing politician Enoch Powell in 1968. And we can, of course, find similar patterned, poised, rhetorical writing in political speeches from all positions on the ideological spectrum: think of Barack Obama's building, climactic 'yes we can' speech, given after he won the Democratic Presidential primary in South Carolina.

There is, we can conclude, nothing necessarily intrinsic to the *stuff* of literature that is any more literary than the stuff of other verbal forms. Literary works do not have to be particularly fancy or ornamental in their language. And conversely, literature's formal properties – rhyme, alliteration, metaphor, sound-patternings and so on – can all be found in non-literary writing too. It seems necessary, then, to look for other ways to get more precisely at the essence of literature, and to say what it is.

Let us return to our poem. It employs, we have said, a pleasurable, sensuous and sonorous kind of language. But, however enjoyable it is, we'd have to say that it is really rather a difficult poem, at least on a first encounter. It seems hard to get at its meaning. And that very fact implies both that it has a meaning and that getting at that meaning is part of what we want from literature. On the other hand, simply to extract the poem's meaning and leave behind its formal, sensuous and sonorous qualities would seem to betray everything that is special about it.

It seems necessary, then, to try to relate the formal, sonorous and sensual aspects of the poem – the *way* it speaks and spells – to its meaning – to *what* it tells us or spells out for us. And when literary critics in Britain and the States first began to suggest general principles for how literature should be analysed, they took precisely this direction. They suggested that literature demands *close reading*. They defined this as an attention to the words on the page: to their interaction and to the relationship between the technical aspects of a work of literature and its message or sense. This approach to literary analysis was called New Criticism in the States, and Practical Criticism in Britain. And from it emerged an implicit definition of literature itself – of literature as a verbal entity which offered a unity of form and meaning. What I'll now do is to offer a close reading of this poem. This will help us at once to understand the poem itself more fully, and to see how 'close reading' *works*. We'll then pause to reflect back on what this might tell us more generally about what literature is, and about the theories of the critics who suggest that we should read it in this way.

# Close Reading and New Criticism

In general terms, this poem expresses two separate but related ideas, one in the octet – the first eight lines of this Petrarchan sonnet – and the other in the sestet, the following six lines. In the octet the poet captures the bedazzling variety of the world and the uniqueness of every single mortal thing within it. In the sestet he suggests that there is an essence underlying all this variety – that everything is uniquely itself by being part, also, of God.

Having established this general sense, we can now focus in more closely. The octet is implicitly answering a 'what is' question. It is trying to get to and to render – to deal out *for us* – the very essence of kingfisherness, of dragonflyness, of stoneness, of bellness. It wants to express the intimate 'being' which dwells 'indoors' or inside each of these things. What are these things, it asks? They are *themselves*, it replies; each living thing 'speaks and spells' its own name and nature, by fully and constantly enacting its singular qualities.

*How*, though, does the poem go about telling us these things? One of the ways it does this is through metaphor – through describing something as if it was something else. So it is as *if* kingfishers catch fire, blazing blue in the light, shining forth radiant in their own unique plumage. In the same way as the kingfishers catch fire, the iridescent wings of the dragonfly glimmer, *as though* they are drawing flame towards themselves.

The octet then moves from those two visual images to three aural ones – the sound that stones make as they're flung into the well; the sound that stringed instruments make as they're plucked; and the sound a bell makes as its clapper is swung against the metal. Again, it is a case of each thing doing what its essential nature dictates, fulfilling its innermost, unique being. And in each case, that thing's essence is described though metaphor. Odd effects emerge here. Let's start at the end with that last image of the bell – 'Each hung bell's/Bow swung finds tongue to fling out broad its name'. One word for the clapper of a bell is precisely its 'tongue'. That word is a dead metaphor. It's based on the clapper's likeness to a human tongue. So what Hopkins does here is to revive a dead metaphor, making *it* speak out to us once more, just as the clapper of the bell speaks the very name of the bell, precisely through doing what it is that bells are there to do, namely to ring. And that's not all. If we look back at the previous aural images of the stone and the stringed instrument we see that, strangely, a stone, like a bell, rings, and an instrument and a bell, like a person, speak.

Metaphor depends on the resemblance between two things, but also their difference. And Hopkins's *use* of metaphor plays out the poem's guiding notion that all the variegated beauty in the world is underpinned by a fundamental sameness, a divine essence. This idea of a divine essence underlying the world's prodigious variety is fully expressed when we move to the second part of the poem. Here the poet goes one further. 'I say more', he writes. Leaping over the gap between octet and sestet, the poem performs also a leap of faith; and Hopkins's *saying more* is a profession of that faith. All the beautiful diversity and uniqueness he has been celebrating resolves itself here into simplicity, played out, in the last three lines at least, in a greater simplicity of diction. And the simplicity is that of the incarnation. Underlying all that variegated individuality is a fundamental, Godly identity, pointed towards in the octet, but now given His name: God.

More minutely, too, the patterning of the poem's sounds jibe with this overarching sense. In the first line, those hard 'c's catch in your throat, and cause you to propel the words, to *fling them out*, 'going yourself' as a reader as you realize, too, the poem's own message and nature. There are overlapping waves of sound, each stage of the poem arising out of possibilities latent in what went before, so that the 'f's in the first half of the first line – 'as kingfishers catch fire' – are repeated in the middle of 'dragonfly', and then the 'r's in 'dragonfly' and 'draw' become the dominant sound in 'rim' and 'roundy', and 'stones ring' rings in 'tucked string'. It might almost seem that the poem generates *itself*, out of the generous fecundity of the language: but ultimately, the 'f' which flares up and flaunts itself throughout the first line returns, at its close, 'to the Father'. These alliterative chains and continuities suggest, then, in keeping with Hopkins's theological message, that there *is* a larger thread uniting all the multiplicity and diversity it celebrates.

We don't have to believe in (a Christian) God to read this sonnet, but its movement and form show us how the poet imagines Him. Just as the almost mad proliferation of images and metaphors in the octet, piling up on one another in a frenzy of similarity and difference, is contained by the sonnet structure, with its fixed number of lines, its division into octet and sestet and its rhyme scheme, so everything is, finally, held in place by God, who is outside the temporal, dynamic play of the world, but, through Christ, participates in it too.

We have shown, then, how the poem works by tracing a series of interrelations between what it says and how it says it; between its craft and its meaning, its form and its content, its sound and its sense. We have offered, in short, a close reading of it. When we are taught to read literature (and especially, but not solely, poetry) we are often inducted into the arts of this kind of analysis. As I've said, it has its origins in the principles laid down for the teaching of literature in British and American universities, from the 1920s to the early 1960s, by critics who came to be known as the 'New Critics' or exponents of 'practical criticism'. (The institutional histories of these schools of criticism are outlined more fully in my introduction). Out of the need to teach literature, and justify the autonomous discipline of literary studies, there evolved a theory of reading and literature which promoted precisely the kind of literary criticism we have just performed on Hopkins's poem. It represents an attempt to study literature on its own terms – to focus and tighten the study of it, and to exclude from consideration things that don't pertain to its existence *as literature*. New Criticism deliberately excluded from its considerations anything seen as extrinsic to the literary work itself: the biography of its author, that author's stated intentions and the text's historical context. The New Critic W.K. Wimsatt, in an essay directed explicitly at university English teachers entitled 'What to Say About a Poem' (1963), says that the aim of literary analysis should be 'the achievement of a valid account of the relation between poetic form and poetic meaning' (1965, 244). Our close reading of the poem offered just such an account, and – as I hope you'll agree – it did elicit many of its qualities and shed some light on them. But when Wimsatt describes the process of this kind of close literary analysis, he does so in terms which make bigger and more abstract claims for it. Here is where we need to pay a more *theoretical* attention to the implications of the New Critical project. Wimsatt writes:

> We begin to talk about patterns of meaning; we encounter structures or forms which are radiant or resonant with meaning. Patterns and structures involve coherence (unity, coherence, and emphasis), and coherence is an aspect of truth and significance. (240)

Wimsatt's discussion of the close reading of a poem moves from a description of what happens in a guided seminar-room encounter with a poem's forms and meaning to a rather grander profession of faith in truth and unity. He implies that the best literature *ought* in some ways to perform in its form and craft what it posits in its content – that literature just is a melding of form and meaning in which each supports the other, and the two together give us truth. It's as though each work of literature, through fulfilling itself to the utmost, through 'radiating' and 'resonating', also manifests the truth. What's rather odd is that his literary theory is strangely similar to Hopkins's theology, in which each mortal thing, by being itself, simultaneously participates in divine Truth.

Literary theorists who work from different intellectual positions – such as the Marxist Terry Eagleton – suggest that this is no mere coincidence. Eagleton writes that 'if one were asked to provide a single explanation for the growth of English studies in the later nineteenth century, one could do worse than reply: "the failure of religion" ' (Eagleton, 22). He implies that literature – in an increasingly secular society – comes to fulfil the ideological roles, and personal needs, that religion no longer provides. For Eagleton, there is, then, a hidden agenda implicitly at work in the installation of literature as a subject for academic study. In view of this argument, we might ask whether the New Critics haven't simply transposed a Christian belief in the unity of the world onto literature, giving us a theology and an ideology of literature rather than *its* truth. Wimsatt's discussion of the process of literature certainly seems to tend in that direction. More generally, this sense of an implicit agenda can prompt us to question the truth of New Criticism's grander claims. Is all literature *necessarily* a beautiful fusion of form and meaning? Might not literature equally well, for example, pull itself apart, trip itself up, be at odds with itself? Might certain forms, such as the novel, just be too baggy to unite form and meaning in the way a sonnet can?

## Testing New Criticism's claims

We can pursue our questions into the more general theoretical claims implicitly made by New Critics such as Wimsatt, by looking at other works of literature. Let's take a poem often quoted by the New Critics themselves, Archibald MacLeish's 'Ars Poetica' (1925). It begins:

> A poem should be palpable and mute
> As a globed fruit

and ends

> A poem should not mean
> But be.

The opening to the poem articulates, in words which we can't touch or palpate, the 'truth' that a poem should be palpable and mute, should not use words at all. The abstract meaning we derive from this poem – that a poem shouldn't mean but have a physical, organic, feelable existence – is at odds with the fact that it *has* that meaning. MacLeish's meaning either cancels itself out, or else, against other evidence, this is not, after all a poem. This seems to be a poem which is saying, paradoxically, 'this is not a poem'. That a poem contains a paradox does not, however, preclude close reading. Indeed this quite knowing contradiction might demonstrate to us a higher truth – namely that the true essence of poetry is precisely beyond words, since it can only be manifested to us in their self-cancellation and self-sacrifice.

But there are other works of literature which can be read even less easily for their over-arching coherence. Take Annie Proulx's short story 'Brokeback Mountain' (1997), which we'll read in chapter 5 in order to explore the pleasures it delivers and what it says about pleasure. The moral and narrative thrust of Proulx's story suggests quite repressively that we can't just take our pleasures where we want. Its concluding sentence – 'if you can't fix it, you've got to stand it' (318) – argues that we should stoically put up with a world we can't change and not be too cavalier about how we take our pleasures within it. Proulx herself said in an interview that this closing sentence expressed the story's moral. And yet – as many readers' responses to the story have shown, and as you may well yourself find if you read it – it is a story which makes itself quite promiscuously available to readers' desires, opening up a polymorphous parade of pleasures even while Proulx prudishly prohibits them. Some of what the story *does*, is at odds with what it most overtly seems to want to *say*. Other literature we'll explore later in this book evinces similar contradictions. As we read Dickens's novel *Hard Times* (1854) in chapter 4, one of the questions we will ask is whether Dickens's overt political message coheres at all junctures with how he conveys that message. And in the next chapter, we will wonder whether Conrad's 'The Secret Sharer' (1909) *has* a 'message' or determinable 'content' at all.

There are a number of cases, then, when literature seems not quite to offer the sublime communion of form and meaning which a New Critical approach to it might seek. Literature, we must conclude, need not cohere organically. And sometimes the pleasure we take in it lies in the fact that it doesn't.

None of this is to suggest that it is wrong or invalid to offer close readings however. As we've seen, such a reading can disclose all sorts of important things about a work of literature, and elicit in nuanced ways many of its qualities and felicities. Moreover, it is only by reading a text closely that we can discern the elements in it which *don't* cohere. The problem comes when critics seize on the *possibility* that literature might unite form and meaning, and offer this as a general way of defining all that literature is, or all one should look for in it. Close reading can't be discarded or simply superceded. But it might be helpful to look at other ways of answering our guiding question as to what literature *is*.

## Russian Formalism: making strange

Preceding but overlapping with the period when Anglo-American critics were developing their ideas about literature as a union of form and meaning, critics in Russia also turned their attention to the *formal* aspects of works of literature. Such critics came to be known as 'Russian Formalists' – though, as with many names and identifications of literary 'schools', this is a designation given after the fact. These critics – writing between 1914 and 1930, after which their work was suppressed by Stalinism – include writers such as Viktor Shklovsky, Boris Eikhenbaum, and Roman Jakobson. While there was little or no communication between the Russian Formalists and the New Critics, they share a similar impulse: to study literature on its own terms, exploring its properties and effects. Unlike the New Critics, however, they emphasize not the *unity* of a work of literature, but rather its estranging properties.

To clarify this we can look at a quotation from Victor Shklovsky. It's from a famous early essay called 'Art as Technique' (1916) or in an alternative translation 'Art as Device'. Its title suggests, then, the technical or artificial aspects of literature, rather than – as with the New Critics – its organic wholeness.

> The technique of art is to make objects 'unfamiliar', to make forms difficult, to increase the difficulty and length of percep-tion because the process of perception is an aesthetic end in itself and must be prolonged. (12)

Shklovsky is proposing that what literature does is to make things strange, to *defamiliarize* them, to use a word translated from the Russian *ostranenie*. To explain what this means, we can return to our kingfishers. The initial description of them catch-ing fire brings us up short, makes us attend to the act of looking at a kingfisher again. We see them in a new light. More gener-ally – as we registered when we first broached it – the poem cannot easily be assimilated to our usual ways of reading or understanding. It takes a long while for us to make the poem our own. And it therefore demands that we tarry with it *as* a poem – that we don't close too quickly on its meaning, but think about how its meanings are made, and – therefore – how we usually make sense of the world ourselves. 'As kingfishers catch fire' both deforms and extends the language, re-inventing it, making it perform as never before, and consequently exhorting its reader to do likewise and, in the process, to become a better reader. Reading the poem in this way takes you out of yourself and, potentially, transforms you. Its estranging linguistic violence, its compaction and inventiveness, its revelling in language's sonorous, material, non-meaningful properties, and its induction of the reader into a world in which everything has undergone a 'seachange into something rich and strange', all manifest what Shklovsky sees as literature's essential *function* – its capacity to defamiliarize the world and our perception of it.

Alongside the effect on our perception of the world, defamil- iarizing language also foregrounds itself. In order to make us see the world anew, such literary language has to be more obtrusive than everyday writing or speaking. It  takes us out into the world, forcing us to re-see it – but it does that by, at precisely the same time, pointing also to its own action. It has, therefore, a *self*-referential quality. Another Russian Formalist, Roman Jakobson, puts this property succinctly, in his essay 'What is Poetry' (1934):

> Poeticity is present when the word is felt as a word and not a mere representation of the object being named or an outburst of emotion, when words and their composition, their meaning, their external and inner form acquire a weight and value of their own instead of referring indifferently to reality. (Jakobson 1987, 378)

Poetic language, as well as taking us out into the world, making us look afresh at kingfishers and dragonflies, also takes us back to *itself*, its own literariness and the very language it employs. In the very act of shocking us into looking at the kingfisher we attend to *how Hopkins is presenting* the kingfisher, and so we are forced to attend to the language in which he renders this. His use of alliteration flaunts itself and its own artifice. Here we might make a point about the well-known literary device of alliteration. Whatever more local literary effects alliteration might have – and sometimes it might be nothing but pure perversity or a puerile pleasure in play – what it always does is to draw attention to literature's own very matter, the stuff it's made of, language and indeed the very matter of language, the letter itself.

## Testing the Russian Formalists' claims

The Russian Formalists offer a definition not so much of literature as of what we might call *literariness* – the property *in* literature that *makes* it literature. Literariness is the capacity literature has at once to make us re-see the world, by interrupting our usual, habitual modes of perception, and to flag up and reflect upon its own very being, its own whatness.

We might ask sceptical questions here once more. Are these qualities of defamiliarization and of self-referentiality, this shocking flaunting of what it is doing, to be found in all literature? It is quite easy to point to them in Hopkins's sonnet. My choice of example has perhaps loaded the dice. But what about, for example, a realist novel? The language of realist novels claims, after all, just to be pointing to the world. Let's look at a bit of one. This is the moment in Elizabeth Gaskell's *Mary Barton* (1848) in which she is describing the interior of a working class home:

> The room was tolerably large, and possessed many conveniences. On the right of the door, as you entered, was a longish window, with a broad ledge. On each side of this, hung blue-and-white check curtains, which were now drawn, to shut in the friends met to enjoy themselves. (13)

There's no drawing attention here, it might seem, to the wordiness of the words themselves. It's more like a mirror, than a self-conscious work of art. And that is the illusion that realist writing always depends on – its very aim is to *efface* its own literariness and artifice, and to make us forget that we are reading fiction. Gaskell's language is very precise – it describes things minutely in terms of their size, their spatial disposition, their colour and so on. It seems to be very purely referential – to be referring directly to things in the world. As twenty-first century readers we are very used to this kind of realist writing – our eye passes over it quite easily, we assimilate its meanings with little resistance. It does not defamiliarize.

But imagine reading *Mary Barton* when it was published, in 1848. This is the year when a wave of revolutions was sweeping Europe. It's also when Chartists in Britain were arguing for universal male suffrage. And in literary-historical terms, the form of the novel at this moment was still actively defining itself against the more fantastical genre of the romance. In those contexts, a middle-class reader of Gaskell's novel might indeed have found its measured mirroring of a working-class home defamiliarizing. In such contexts, the passage might well have been read as saying quite deliberately *look* at how calm and measured I'm being in my description of a working class home; *look* at how I'm mirroring things without obtruding myself; *look,* in short, at how superbly realistic I'm being. In certain *contexts* then, and read with a different set of assumptions than ours in mind, Gaskell's novel might, indeed, appear to make the world and literature strange.

These arguments take us beyond the province of Russian Formalist theories themselves, though they are opened up *by* them. Russian Formalists, in their accounts of defamiliarization, tend to privilege very specific, overtly strange, kinds of writing. Shklovsky, in demonstrating how literature can disrupt our 'automated' forms of perception, gives the example of a Tolstoy short story, 'Kholstomer' in which events are narrated from the point of view of a horse. This strange point of view makes ordinary human assumptions emerge as odd, ideological beliefs. The horse reflects, for instance, on the human word 'my' as it is applied to him: 'my horse'. What does it mean to talk about living beings in terms of property? What does it mean, indeed, to think of oneself as owning 'property'? Again we can see the effects of defamiliarization here. But what Shklovsky – and other Russian Formalists such as Jakobson – don't really ask about is *whose* perception is being defamiliarized. After all, if 'Kholstomer' were read in a culture in which there *was* no private property, the horse's reflections would not be challenging its reader's assumptions in the same way.

In short, then, Russian Formalists don't really address the question of the *contexts* in which defamiliarization might operate, or the nature of the *reader* who would register its effects. In terms of our guiding question – what is literature? – they therefore imply that literature is *essentially* defamiliarizing, but never make good on this claim. They ignore literature's context and its reader – aspects on which other theorists focus their attention more explicitly. We'll look at those in just a moment. Before we do, it will be helpful to pause and reflect a bit more on the very terms of our what-is-literature question.

When we ask what something is, we imply *that* it is: that it has an essence or an identity that we can enquire into. Our question implies, that, ultimately, we will be able to say 'literature is [such and such a thing]'. Accompanying the work of much literary theory, however, is a questioning of the very idea of identity or essence. In the next, brief, section of this chapter, I'm going to pull back from explicit theories of literariness in order to explain more fully questions of essence and identity. Such questions are helpful for engaging with any aspect of literary theory, but they also bear directly on our guiding question in this chapter.

# The 'what is?' question

Let's look at Hopkins's sonnet once more. The poem itself stages questions of essence and whatness. Elsewhere, and borrowing from the theologian Duns Scotus, Hopkins calls this *haeccitas* – the God-given 'thisness' of something. Here Hopkins asks about the 'thisness' – the essence – of each mortal thing. What makes things what they uniquely are? His answer, as we have seen, is two fold. Everything, he says, is both itself and God. In giving us this answer, he also shows us things about the assumptions and beliefs behind the 'what is' question. For a start, he suggests that at the heart of each being is an essence, a fundamental quality or nature, which it just is. Everything has, for Hopkins, a God-given nature. Just by being itself it manifests that nature. But second, and slightly differently, the being of life in fact inheres also in what mortal things *do*, in their acts, functions, in their *goings*. To be is not to sit still, but to keep acting, doing, going, saying, to *keep* being oneself. Here 'being' is understood as a *process* rather than a fixed essence. Third, in order to deal out for *us* the 'being' of all things, Hopkins has to describe them in terms of other things, to place them in a set of relationships in which their unique differences *and* their similarities can be experienced. Hopkins's use of metaphor and analogy demonstrates this.

Thus Hopkins's poem gives us three different answers to what or how something is. In the first case, he suggests that everything has a deep-down essence. In the second, he suggests that its nature inheres in what it does rather than what it is. In the third, he allows us to think (though it is not, perhaps, his own belief) that the existence of things is *contextual* or *relational*.

We can see how this might be related productively to our question 'what is literature?' and help sharpen it up. Do we want to find out the 'essence' of literature – its fixed, deep-down property? The New Critical position seemed to be essentialist in this way, implying that literature just *is* the unity of form and meaning. But it was easy to find instances which contradicted that claim. The Russian Formalists took a more functional approach, suggesting that literariness was a question of what literature *did* – the way it worked in the world. Illuminating though their arguments are, what they don't address is the nature of the world – the contexts in which literature might intervene and make strange. Here, then, is where a more *contextual* argument might be helpful. Literature does not exist in a vacuum, but in its relationship to other things – to its contexts and its readership. These are aspects of the 'what is literature?' question explored more thoroughly by historicist and reader response theorists. They suggest – in a terminology utterly alien to Hopkins – that literature has no inherent *haeccitas*, thisness or essence, but is a *construct*.

## Context

Let's return here to our passage from Elizabeth Gaskell's *Mary Barton*. In many ways, both the defamiliarizing shock of what she writes – it's startlingly life-like – and its effect therefore of remarking its own realism, come about because this sort of gritty realism is a contested form of writing in the mid-nineteenth century. The novel at this moment is in the process of defining itself against the earlier, still enduring, form of romance – a form which precisely doesn't aim at a reality-effect. There are many discussions happening at this time about what the proper mode and matter of literature *ought* to be – whether it ought, for example, to be engaged in representing the working classes and their homes in the first place, or whether it oughtn't to be dealing with more elevated topics. We can see this by placing Gaskell's words into relationship with a passage from George Eliot's *Adam Bede* (1859), where the narrator pulls out of the story she is telling, in order to make a direct claim for what literature ought to be able to contain:

> Paint us an angel if you can [...], paint us yet oftener a Madonna [...] but do not impose on us any aesthetic rules which shall banish from the region of Art those old women scraping carrots with their work-worn hands, those heavy clowns taking holiday in a dingy pot-house, those rounded backs and stupid weather-beaten faces that have bent over the spade and done the rough work of the world, those houses with their tin pans, their brown pitchers, their rough curs and their clusters of onions. (224)

Gaskell's novel makes no such overt – and overtly self-referential – claims. Her writing quietly gets on with what it is doing. But it only does what it does, and is what it is, as a consequence of the contexts in which it is written. It cannot exist in a glorious self-sufficiency – its being is in great part dependent on its relationships to other events, discussions, texts and contexts. It tells us what it's doing partly by dint of what it's *not* doing. This is why, against the apparent evidence, we may still suggest that it defamiliarizes – its own realism flaunts itself, marking it out as 'strange' in relation to more 'romantic' representations of the world which exclude details of working-class life from their province.

We can suggest, then, that what literature is understood to be changes at different moments in its history, and any particular work that flags up its 'literariness' will depend on the contexts of debates about what literature *is* in which it intervenes. These *historicist* arguments open up a whole range of questions about how we should read literature in relation to its context – questions which deserve separate attention, and which we'll therefore go on to discuss in chapter 4.

For now, pursuing our explicit question 'what is literature?', we can think about these questions in terms of the role of the *reader.* To think of a text marking out its own literariness in relationship to its contexts, is to consider its effects on a contemporary reader – and also to open the question as to how it might be read at different historical moments. There has to be someone there to receive and remark a text's nature and way of being, just as, in Hopkins's poem, man is only what he is through being seen 'in God's eye'. But a reader is not God-like. She exists in a particular place and time, and comes to a text with a whole load of personal baggage, as well as with various inherited or culturally acquired assumptions about what literature is.

# The reader and 'reader-response' theory

A number of thinkers writing in Germany in the 1960s and the United States in the 1970s and 80s, turned their attention explicitly to the importance of the *reader* and of *reception* in literary criticism, and formulated theories about how literary writing was read and received. They include Wolfgang Iser and Hans Robert Jauss, German 'reception' theorists, and Stanley Fish and David Bleich, American 'reader–response' theorists. And perhaps the most vocal and provocative of the 'reader–response' theorists, Stanley Fish, turned his attention explicitly to how the reader him or herself is actually engaged in defining what literature *is*.

Fish argues that literature does not have an innate essence. Rather, readers' *assumptions* are what define it. He writes that:

> Literature ... is the product of a way of reading, of a community agreement about what will count as literature... Since that way of reading ... is not eternally fixed but will vary with cultures and times, the nature of the literary institution and its relation to other institutions... will be continually changing. (1980: 97)

According to Fish, then, there's no such thing as an essence of literature. Literature is nothing but a product of cultural decisions about what literature is, and it is produced *by* reading rather than by offering itself to be read. There's a vicious circle where we are taught how to read, by our schools, universities and society and large. The way we're taught is informed by an already-present idea of what literature is. And as we read it, we therefore find what it is we've been taught to look for. Literature is not an essence but a *'construct'* – something made by institutions under the pressure of the particular things they ask of it.

Let's spend a while looking at the evidence in support of Fish's argument. We can return first to another bit of the essay by Wimsatt discussed earlier:

> At the outset what can we be sure of? Mainly that a poem says or means something, or ought to mean something (or ought to if we as teachers have any business with it – perhaps that is the safe minimum). (221)

Wimsatt's humorous series of qualifications demonstrates something rather interesting: namely that he is not in fact entirely 'sure' that all poems mean or ought to mean something. Only, his parenthesis implies, poems *for teaching* need to mean something. An institutional and pedagogical imperative drives his definition of what literature is then. And we might point out that New Critical close reading offers a view of literature rather convenient for class-room teaching. If, after all, reading closely the 'words on the page' is what it's all about, the department can make do with a slim poetry anthology or handouts, rather than having to buy in lots of volumes. Movements in literary criticism and theory *themselves* depend on their context.

I can draw on my own context – I write in the British education system in the first decade of the twenty-first century – for further evidence of this. Government educational policy in Britain over the last two decades has tended to emphasize quantifiable knowledge and skills, whose acquisition can be charted by measuring a student's reading of a poem, novel or play against a number of clearly laid-out 'assessment objectives'. This emphasis – we could argue – is driven by the political requirement to test how schools are functioning, in order to allocate funding appropriately. Last year's (2008) A-S-level examination, for high school students aged seventeen or so, laid out the marks-scheme for an essay on Angela Carter's *Wise Children* as follows: seven marks out of thirty for 'terminology', ten marks for 'knowledge', eight marks for 'structure/meaning' and five marks for 'your opinion'. Literature, according to the implicit set of definitions at work here, is something that requires a particular terminology, can be known, has a structure and a meaning, and is something about which you must have an opinion (but not too much of one). Different examinations offered at the same stage 'test' for different things: a knowledge of 'context', an appreciation of 'critical views' of a text, and so on. We can see very explicitly then how institutions and communities, by approaching literature in specific ways, make literature into what it is they need, in order to measure student success.

As further evidence in favour of Fish's argument we can also point out that what we term 'literature' is different at different historical moments. Students studying Anglo-Saxon or Renaissance literature, for example, might well read Old English sermons or the homilies of John Donne, whereas most exploring the literature of the twentieth century would be rather surprised to find the sermons of modern clerics on their reading lists. And indeed, if we look at the *Oxford English Dictionary* we can see that before about 1800, the word 'literature' was used to mean any kind of writing or book learning. Its modern sense – which we use all the time, though we have not yet in this chapter arrived at a satisfactory definition of it – is, then, a very recent invention.

*Ways* of reading literature also change over time. The things we might expect to find in 'As Kingfishers Catch Fire' today might well be different from those its contemporary readers sought. Hopkins's friend and editor Robert Bridges, introducing the first edition of his poems, sees fit to put his readers 'at their ease' by defining the vices we will find in his poetry – 'they may be called Oddity and Obscurity' he writes, and continues, 'since the first may provoke laughter when a writer is serious (and this poet is always serious), while the latter must prevent him from being understood (and this poet has always something to say), it may be assumed that they were not a part of his intention' (Bridges, 96). How very different from the way you might read the poem if you approached it having read some Victor Shklovsky! You might then – as we have done here – understand its estranging Oddity as a virtue rather than a vice, seeing it as the way in which the poem is *being itself* by foregrounding in a particularly vivid manner literature's capacity always to be a bit Odd. But, if we follow Fish, this reading would be no truer than Bridges': it would simply be a function of the fact that, as a twenty-first-century reader who has begun to read some literary theory, you have internalized Formalist ideas.

Much, then, might be said in support of Fish's argument. 'Literature' is a product of how we read it – but this is by no means to say that each individual one of us can decide what we want literature to be. Quite the reverse, in fact, because for Fish we read in the ways in which we've been taught to read – at school and university and also by our culture at large and the historical moment in which we live. This seems, up to a point, to be undeniable. There is no reading without our being taught to read, and no existence that can simply lift itself out the mesh of social and cultural relationships in which it exists. Hopkins's sonnet starts with an 'as' – inaugurating us from the start into a world of *likenesses*.

But there's nevertheless something rather fishy going on in Fish's argument. We might describe it as a strange displacement. Often, we understand literature to be a kind of fictional writing. Here, the fiction is said to be not *in literature* but outside it. The fiction, for Fish, is precisely the fact that we understand there to be a single, trans-historical, trans-cultural thing called literature in the first place. Literature's fire, flame and force are removed from it, and attributed, instead, to culture, to institutions, to history. *As* literature makes things up, implies Fish, so too do our culture and schooling: and what they make up is what literature is. 'Literariness' now seems to be everywhere but the place in which we usually expect to find it. The last section of this chapter will consider some responses to this strange situation.

# Cultural studies and deconstruction: literature's futures

One response to theoretical arguments such as Fish's, which accord to culture many of the properties we expect to find in literature, is to transfer our literary-critical skills *to* culture and to read *it*. This approach has led to a growing discipline known as 'cultural studies'. There is some excellent work in this field. You might find interesting, for example, Clare Birchall's *Knowledge goes Pop: From Conspiracy Theory to Gossip* (2006), a book which 'reads' public responses to and 'theories' about events like Princess Diana's death and the attacks on the World Trade Center on 11 September 2001. Exploring the popular stories that sprang up in the media, on the internet and in everyday conversations about these events, Birchall argues that 'conspiracy theory' is 'a narrative construct that allows readers to rewrite or re-cognize events' (44). She argues, then, that ways of talking about world and cultural events are themselves acts of reading and rewriting which can themselves be reread and re-interpreted. Literariness goes pop and global here, and the skills literary critics have evolved in order to respond to litera-ture, and the theories about what literature is and how it works which attend their endeavours, find new applications.

But if all this is the case – well, it suggests that literature 'itself' still has something to teach us, and cannot *only* be understood as a symptom of culture, best understood by giving up on literature and turning to the society which 'writes' it. We might think back to Carter's *Wise Children*. British students are taught that this work of literature is something that can be *known*. But to know *Wise Children* is to have to read it. And to read it is to encounter the lively and idiomatic narrative voice of Dora Chance, and through it to experience an irreverent, 'wrong side of the tracks' (1) way of reading literature itself. Dora, the chorus-girl and illegitimate twin daughter of Melchior Hazard, an actor famous for playing all the greatest Shakespearean roles, is steeped in the language of Shakespeare. This is one of the 'cultures' she has been born into, and it shapes her language and thoughts – as it does, indeed, those of her readers throughout English-speaking parts of the world. When Dora or we use the popular cliché 'discretion is the better part of valour', we are alluding, in our case possibly unknowingly, to Falstaff's comically callow dictum 'the better part of valour is discretion' from Shakespeare's *Henry IV Part One* (5. 4. 118). And Carter's novel as a whole multiply manifests the ways in which it, too, exists in a 'post-Shakespearean' culture, in its five-part 'dramatic' structure, its comic use of multiple sets of twins, and so on. Simply to juxtapose – as Fish does – cultural 'institutions' *to* the literature they 'produce' is to ignore the ways in which culture, language, society and so on arise in part *from* prior acts of reading.

Dora, having been shaped by her reading, and by these prior acts of reading is not, however, the simple dupe of her culture which a theorist like Fish imagines. She is able to use her readings of Shakespeare to re-interpret and reread the world in which she lives. When she writes, for example, of the dreamy atmosphere which takes over the whole cast of the Hollywood production of *A Midsummer Night's Dream*, 'we were all spell-bound now', she is using her intimate knowledge of the play to convey the way a kind of midsummer madness can seize a group of people working closely together, causing precisely the kinds of delirium and confused identities which Shakespeare in his play attributes to magic. Dora, in her approach to Shakespeare, is at once utterly faithful to each of the plays, and yet also responds to them in singular ways, offering what the theorist and novelist Hélène Cixous, in her book *So Close* (2009) calls a 'pirate reading', carrying off their unique contraband as treasure for her own use. And so, if a British A-level student of *Wise Children* does 'know' this book, this 'wise child' of twenty-first-century culture will know too that it must be read faithfully and responded to idiomatically and in singular ways. We can only hope the examiner will be equally wise.

This double movement, where we need to know how to read literature in order to read it, but where the singular experience of reading any particular work of literature can at once transform our notion of literature and our culturally-inherited idea of what reading is, can best be described as the movement of 'deconstruction'. It was first named as such by Jacques Derrida. In an aptly entitled interview, 'This strange institution called literature' (Derrida 1992), he suggests that 'literature perhaps stands on the edge of everything, almost beyond everything, including itself' (47). This almost-unimaginable topography helps us see why, in this chapter, we have been able to shuttle backwards and forwards between the singularity of Hopkins's sonnet, and our own pressing question about what literature, in general, *is*. Almost every time I have outlined some definition of the literary, I have said not only that the sonnet might be said to *display* some of those literary qualities – but that it might, in some sense, also be said to be talking about them.

There is a peculiar sort of Tardis-effect, whereby our theoretical, philosophical, historical and so on comments on the literary object seem already to have been made *by* it. The poem's 'outside' – all these theoretical discourses about literature – seem already to be on its inside. And one of the questions it takes into its inside is that of whether it could be said to *have* an inside – whether it has a 'being' that dwells indoors of itself. But these effects are only visible insofar as we respond to and read the poem, put questions to it, and ask what other things 'As Kingfishers Catch Fire' might be considered *as*, allowing it to 'catch fire' with reflected light.

Literature – when we read it – can help us think about what happens when we ask that philosophical question 'what is?'. Indeed it seems that, if *asking* 'what is?' is a philosophical question, *saying* what something is, is actually a strange, and quite literary, business. As the reader and theorist of Freud, Cixous and Derrida, Sarah Wood, claims, in a singular reading of Elizabeth Bowen's *The Little Girls* (1963) called 'Try Thinking As If Perhaps ...', 'literature offers the most advanced way of thinking about thinking' (2004, 159).

## Singularity

Wood's article offers a beautifully odd reading of Bowen and of Derrida. As she suggests, and other readers and theorists of literature and of Derrida such as Derek Attridge (2004), Timothy Clark (2005) and Peggy Kamuf (1997) also, and differently, articulate, literature offers the promise of always-singular encounters. As Derek Attridge puts it 'the singularity of the work ... speaks to my own singularity' (78). It does this because, while it draws on the general possibilities inherent in the language, and there in the context from which it emerges, it always reframes, reinvents and reflects on these, dislocating them and constellating them anew. In doing so it calls for a response – a reader's response. Readers, too, exist in contexts, and can't simply escape these. But the give and flexibility in literary writing suggest that there is flexibility in context too – to read is always to inhabit another's time and place, and so the very possibility of reading and of writing marks out the fact that the constraints of my own time and culture are not absolutely determining. According to this 'deconstructive' reading, literature is not an essence so much as a possibility – a possibility that can always be missed. What it does is to demand from us a response which is just and faithful without being Jesuitical. Such a response would attest to all that is singular about a literary text, through registering also the singularity of our own response to it – the way that it addresses us and summons us from our own particular place and time.

Because of this, no *general* answer to our guiding question is possible. The answer will always emerge from a specific context of reading and response. On the other hand, any answer that we give, from the place in which we are reading, might always be more generally helpful and inspiring. And so it is possible to offer an answer, based on the singularity of Hopkins's poem and my reading of it here. 'The just man justices' writes the Jesuit Hopkins. He describes here what St Paul, in his letter to the Ephesians, calls grace – the way in which God the father gives to his children the capacity justly to reflect back to him his own glory through a constant perfecting of their own God-given natures. Thanks to Hopkins's sonnet, and to a whole welter of other literary-theoretical readings, writings and reflections, I find myself, as an atheist woman, able to offer a tentative answer to the question 'what is literature?'. Whether my answer is just you must decide for yourself. Literature – I suggest – is a kind of grace, though not a grace that comes from any single father. It is a 'wise child', after all, who knows her own father. Literature glories in its mixed parentage, and multiple offspring, amongst whom as readers, we may include ourselves.

# 3

# What's it mean?

*This* is a question that, at some time or another, has probably been asked by every reader. Literature does not always share its secrets easily. Sometimes there is even a mystique about it. We feel we have to cast our nets wide, or surf the internet, to discover what our text 'really means'. In this chapter we'll read a short story by Joseph Conrad called 'The Secret Sharer' (1911), alongside the writings of a number of theorists who discuss meaning, authorial intention, interpretation and signification. We'll explore what it means to ask what someone or something means, and also ask whether 'what's it mean?' is quite the right question to be asking.

I've chosen 'The Secret Sharer' because the pleasure of reading it lies in part in the ways it seems to tease us with mysterious just-out-of-reach meanings, inciting us to read and reread in order to unlock its secrets. Because it is *about* secrets and secrecy it also offers us what Paul de Man, a theorist of rhetoric and reading, has called 'allegories of reading' (de Man 1979): moments in which reading, interpretation and the divining of meaning take place within the story itself. It's worth focusing on such moments when we read any literature, and asking what they can tell us about how we are being instructed to read, or conversely encouraged not to read.

What, then, is the 'The Secret Sharer' about? Only reading it can really tell you that but I'll begin by giving you a brief account of the plot:

'The Secret Sharer' is the story of a strange event which befalls a young captain as he assumes command of his ship for the first time. The nameless captain – who narrates the story –

tells us how, keeping watch on the first night at sea, miles from land, he is startled to be hailed by a swimmer. The swimmer, whose name is Leggatt, has come from the ship the *Sephora*, where he was chief mate. But he has a dark secret, which he shares with the captain: he has killed a crew-member. He recounts how, escaping imprisonment, he then jumped ship, preferring to swim until he drowned rather than surrender to justice once the *Sephora* reached shore. Our narrator-captain feels an instant affinity for Leggatt, describing him as his double. He hides him in his bedroom, sharing it with him secretly and without the knowledge of his men. He even covers for Leggatt when the captain of the *Sephora* comes looking for him. Finally, at great risk to his ship, and endangering the lives of his discon-certed and suspicious crew, the captain is able to sail close enough to land to allow Leggatt to escape. Using Leggatt's hat, left drifting in the sea, as a marker, he manages at the last minute to bring his ship about to safety and to continue his journey.

So there we have it. But what, you may still ask, does it mean? Despite the fact that I've done the unpardonable and given away the ending, so that it might seem that there's no point in your reading it now, in many ways the story's secret remains intact. Many interesting questions are left unanswered. What does Conrad mean us to think of the captain's decision to harbour a murderer? Who *is* 'The Secret Sharer': the captain who shares his cabin secretly with Leggatt or Leggatt who shares his secret with the captain? And what are we supposed to make of the mysterious Leggatt?

These questions ask what the story is about in a profounder sense than the simple recounting of its plot can reach. They quest for what we think of as its 'deeper' meanings. What *is* the text's secret? Where is it? And how do we go about getting at it? In what follows, we'll look at three possible keepers of the story's secret – the author, the words and structure of the story itself, and the reader. In each case we will appeal to specific theoretical ideas about how these three things might surrender, elicit, harbour or produce the story's meaning, and tease out the meanings and implications of these theories themselves.

# Biographical criticism

Throughout the history of literary criticism, attempts have been made to relate an author's life to their work. In his collection of essays on Jane Austen *Regulated Hatred* written in 1940, D. W. Harding identifies Fanny Price, the heroine of *Mansfield Park* as a 'Cinderella figure' and makes parallels with Austen's own familial situation, as a 'poor relation', dependent on her wealthy brother's charity, and also as a younger sister, often in the shadow of the older Cassandra. In 1989, Louise de Salvo's *Virginia Woolf: The Impact of Childhood Sexual Abuse on her Work,* draws a series of very direct links between Woolf's childhood experiences and her later writing. Anyone who writes or talks about literature confronts the question of how helpful, or legitimate, it is to bring a knowledge of an author's life to bear on an interpretation of their work. What status should we give an author's biography in our attempt to discern his or her meaning?

In the case of the Polish-born Joseph Conrad (aka Konrad Korzeniowski) it's well known that he spent twenty years as a sailor before becoming a novelist. We can see his intimate knowledge of shipboard life and nautical navigation displayed on every page of 'The Secret Sharer'. Moreover one of the main aspects of the story, as he tells us in his 'Author's Note' (1920), came from a real event, albeit one he only read about in a court report. The report told of a man indicted for the murder of the chief mate of the *Cutty Sark* in 1882. There's an obvious resemblance to Leggatt's 'secret' history here.

So there are a number of connections we can draw between Conrad the man and his story. But how do these help us in our quest to say what it means? We already know that it is about a murderer. The fact that this murderer had a 'real life' double doesn't really enable us to decipher what Conrad meant Leggatt to represent. Conrad himself, in his 'Author's Note', suggests that the effect of his own experiences on his writing is far less 'precise' than a one-to-one correspondence between the events in the story and real, historical happenings. He writes that the story is not the record of personal experience as such, but that its 'quality, such as it is, depends on something larger if less precise: on the character, vision, and sentiment of the first twenty independent years of my life' (Conrad 1982, 10). It would seem foolish as well as presumptuous to disagree with this. But we must ask how it helps us. To understand the 'quality' of 'The Secret Sharer' (which is perhaps not quite the same as its meaning) we would have to read extensively, exploring memoirs, letters, diaries and other documents pertaining to the period and Conrad's life and experiences within it. And we wouldn't just have to know the facts of Conrad's life, but would have to read them, offering suggestions as to what *they* mean too. Of course, there are scholars who have recovered many of these facts and already interpreted them, giving us biographies of him (see Stape 2006 and Najder 2007). But biographies, too, need to be read and interpreted. Moreover, as Conrad suggests, reading about his life and contexts might elicit something about the 'quality' of his story, such as the shipboard atmosphere it conveys, but it can't actually tell us what the story means. An author's biography might illuminate aspects of an author's work, then, but it will never actually give us its meaning.

## Authorial intentions

Sometimes, however, authors make more specific statements of their intentions, in their diaries, for example, or in letters to friends. And the extent to which we should take 'authorial intention' into account as we read a work – and the question of how we go about divining that intention – is a subject hotly debated by literary theorists from the 1950s onwards. We'll begin with 'The Secret Sharer', reading Conrad's own statements as to what he intended in writing the story, before considering in a more 'theoretical' way the nature and importance of intention itself.

There are three moments in his *Letters* where Conrad explicitly discusses 'The Secret Sharer'. In the first, writing curtly to his agent Pinker, he says: 'I wrote it for the very purpose of easing the strain. This is all I have to say on my side' (Conrad 1983–2007, 4, 303). So he did it for the money. This is hardly illuminating. Indeed we might wonder whether it is worth continuing to ponder the story's 'deeper meanings' if Conrad's main motivations in writing it were financial. But perhaps we should read on.

In the second letter, to his friend and fellow writer John Galsworthy, he gets angry at what he perceives as *mis*readings of the character of Leggatt, railing against those critics who describe Leggatt as a 'murderous ruffian' (Conrad 1983–2007, 5, 121). It seems clear, then, that this is *not* how we are meant to read Leggatt, even if such a reading, as the critics demonstrate, is still possible. Dismissing this bad reading he continues: 'I meant him to be what you have seen at once he was' (122). And that is that. Just as we seem to home in on Leggatt's 'true' meaning it's snatched away from us. If we want to find it out we then have to read Galsworthy's letter too. And, as I discovered when I tried to, it's not published. We'd have to travel to the Brandeis library in Massachusetts, where Galsworthy's unpublished letters are kept, to read it. This is always a possibility of course, and it may be that the letter will one day be more easily available. For now, though, we have only Conrad's letters.

Third time lucky perhaps. In a letter which covers his views on several of his stories, Conrad writes gleefully to his friend, Edward Garnett:

> On the other hand the Secret Sharer, between you and me, is
> *it*. Eh? No damned tricks with girls there. Eh? Every word fits
> and there's not a single uncertain note. Luck my boy. Pure
> luck. I knew you would spot the thing at sight. But I repeat:
> mere luck. (Conrad 1983–2007, 5, 128)

Once again our hopes of getting any closer to the story's
'meaning' are dashed. Conrad seems here merely to be glorying
in the story's excellence rather than conveying any information
about it. Attempting to find out what Conrad meant by appealing to his own statements about 'The Secret Sharer' seems a
fool's errand.

This is a very specific case of course. While with many works
(Shakespeare's for example) we quite simply don't have any
statements of authorial intention, other writers do – in their
letters or diaries – tell us what they intend to write about, or else
discuss, after they've written it, the meaning of their work. And
more generally, when we read anything – including 'The Secret
Sharer' – we feel that an author has something in mind, and
that the best way to read their work would be to recover what
that is.

In an influential essay called 'The Intentional Fallacy' (1954),
two New Critics, W. K. Wimsatt and Monroe Beardsley, take
on these questions. They suggest that to base our interpretations
on either the explicitly declared, or implicitly intuited, intentions of an author is to work with fallacious assumptions. Basing
their arguments on the public, published and accomplished
nature of a literary work, and asserting that it 'it is detached from
the author at birth and goes about the world beyond his power
to intend about it or control it', they proclaim that 'critical
inquiries are not settled by consulting the oracle' (Wimsatt
1954,18). A text has a separate existence, adrift in the world
without any authorial anchorage. All we must go on, they argue,
are the words of the story (or poem, or play) themselves.

Importantly, Wimsatt and Bearsdley also suggest that even when authors *do* say what they mean, these statements of intention will still have been written at a different moment from the work itself, and will be shaped by pressures other than those which produced the writing. Conrad's letters to Galsworthy and Garnett, for example, have a warmth and jocularity arising from his friendship with each of them, whereas the terse missive to his agent Pinker, with whom he was in bad odour for not finishing his novel *Under Western Eyes* (1911), is more concerned to underscore his financial difficulties and the fact that he is busy trying to resolve them. Statements of authorial intention and the *contexts* in which authors talk about their work need to be read and interpreted too.

In many respects Wimsatt and Beardsley give a helpful caution then. To take an author at their word about their own writing seems to suggest that we could just bypass that writing itself. It ignores the ways in which a text *makes* its meanings, and the craft that went into that making. And it implies a very mechanistic model of what the writing of a story entails. When Conrad writes gleefully to Garnett that the artistic success of 'The Secret Sharer' is 'Luck my boy. Pure luck', he is referring to that exhilarating feeling of everything coming together that sometimes arises when one writes. And he's suggesting, then, that part of the writing was out of his conscious control. He speaks as a delighted reader of his own work after the moment of writing has passed, rather than as someone who had captaincy over it.

Narrowing our reading down to what an author says he meant risks shutting out many of its happy accidents and resonances: aspects of it which come with the writing but weren't necessarily part of any authorial plan. To this extent we can agree, I think, with Wimsatt and Bearsdley. On the other hand, Conrad's sense that the writing came *to* him as a lucky gift, rather than *from* him as a masterful author, must make us wonder about the less knowing, less conscious aspects of authorship. If an author's expressed and conscious intentions are not be trusted, may we not explore their unconscious meanings?

# Psychoanalysis and unconscious meanings

Since the start of the twentieth century, much reading of literature – non-academic and academic alike – has been inflected by the work of Sigmund Freud. (See chapter 5 for a fuller discussion of Freud's writings.) Freud's writings, indeed, have had a profound effect on the whole of twentieth- and twenty-first century culture and thought. Perhaps the most important and influential thing he did was to articulate the idea of the 'unconscious'. For Freud, our everyday conscious actions and what we knowingly intend to do, are governed and often interrupted by unconscious motivations, forces and desires – aspects of our selves that don't fit in with our orderly, civilized existence. The psyche therefore shuts them away from its own knowingness – it represses them.

The well-known idea of the 'Freudian slip' – what Freud called 'parapraxis' or 'mis-saying' – is one example of the unconscious at work. So, for example, when I am attempting to talk in a sober manner about biology, and to refer to an 'organism', and I accidentally say 'orgasm' instead, this suggests that my covert desires are pushing towards expression, hitching a ride on what I consciously want to say, and derailing it for their own ends. Freud writes that 'he that has eyes to see and ears to hear may convince himself that no mortal can keep a secret. If his lips are silent, he chatters with his finger-tips; betrayal oozes out of him at every pore' (Freud 1995, 215).

The 'unconscious', for Freud then, is at once a secret part of the self, unknown to our conscious selves, and yet a part of us that will always push, *against* our intentions, to share its secrets. We are inhabited by a 'secret sharer'. And one way of reading 'The Secret Sharer' itself is as being about the way in which unconscious motivations might govern authorship. Look at this bit, for example:

> I was not wholly alone with my command; for there was that stranger in my cabin. Or rather, I was not completely and wholly with her. Part of me was absent. That mental feeling of being in two places at once affected me physically as if the mood of secrecy has penetrated my very soul. (200)

The captain is in charge of his ship but he doesn't give the job his full attention because he's aware of his 'secret sharer' below decks. In the same way, we might suggest, a writer is responsible for what he writes but isn't fully in control of it either, since his conscious intentions are always being tugged at by unconscious forces. Sometimes unconscious meanings might pull a text in directions other than those in which it seems overtly to want to go. And we might remember that in order to get Leggatt safely ashore at the end of the story, the captain takes his ship wildly off course, and risks it foundering. In his letter to Garnett, however, Conrad suggests that a less doom-laden view of the unconscious is possible too, and that it might harbour more felicitous surprises.

So, an author might not fully *know* his own meaning. Some of it might reside in the unconscious. Our challenge as readers, in that case, would be to dive down to that unconscious meaning. But how do we get at it? Reading Freud's writings, Jacques Derrida suggests that the unconscious 'is not ... a hidden, virtual, or potential self-presence ... [It] sends out delegates, representatives, proxies; but without any chance that the giver of proxies might "exist," might be present, be "itself" somewhere' (Derrida, 1982, 20–1). According to this reading, the unconscious isn't a secret we could just know. And that is certainly the case for us as readers. In order to 'get at' it, all we have to go on are the words of the story. How do we know *which* of the elements of 'The Secret Sharer' are consciously intended by Conrad and which are governed by his unconscious? The story has, for example, a homoerotic or homosocial tug to it. The immediate bond between the two men, the fact of their bedroom sharing, the intimacy of their whispering together, the moment of parting in which their 'hands met gropingly [and] lingered united in a steady motion-less clasp for a second' (211): all this seems to speak of love and attraction. It would betray the story simply to ignore these elements. But to brandish them triumphantly as *the* secret, hidden, singular, unconscious 'meaning' it conveys would be to ignore several things. First it would ignore the fact that Conrad may well have *consciously* intended to suggest a sexual or romantic aspect to the friendship. He himself had several homosexual friends. Second, and more seriously, it would repress all the other ways of reading Leggatt – as, for example, an aspect of the captain's own being, rather than simply a separate person.

To attribute a text's meaning simply to the author's *uncon-scious* intentions would be just as much of a 'fallacy' as the one Wimsatt and Beardsley discern in reading solely for *conscious* intentions. For literary critics the 'delegates, representatives and proxies' of an author's conscious *or* unconscious intentions are his or her words and other marks. Reading them patiently seems the only option.

Repeatedly then, in our discussions of an author's biography, intentions and unconscious motivations, we don't alight at a single meaning, but are returned to the necessity of continued reading. This cannot be a bad thing: as readers, reading is what we do. But it might be helpful for us to think a bit more about what we actually *mean* by reading, and by the word 'meaning' itself.

# The meaning of 'meaning'

The etymologies of the word 'meaning' – those secret roots that link it back to the past and to other languages – are interesting. It's connected to a range of words from Old German and Dutch, meaning to think, to hold a good opinion of, to love and to have in mind. Meaning, then, is linked to minds, to love, to what goes on inside us. And in both his letters to Galsworthy and Garnett, and at certain moments in 'The Secret Sharer', Conrad seems to imagine it in much this way.

In the letter from Conrad to Galsworthy, the latter is credited with having seen 'at once' what Leggatt was. To Garnett, Conrad says that he knew he would 'spot the thing at sight'. And in the 'Secret Sharer' itself, Leggatt tells our captain-narrator his 'story roughly in brusque, disconnected sentences' and the captain comments 'I needed no more' (181–2). Just as Galsworthy and Garnett immediately apprehend what the story is about, so the narrator says, 'I saw it all going on as though I were myself inside that other sleeping-suit' (182). In all three cases, Conrad represents the divining of meaning as an instant, intimate and intuitive understanding, which does not need ponderous explanation. It is as though the readings of the story by the captain, Galsworthy and Garnett offer us 'allegories of reading', which imagine reading as a kind of secret sharing.

Of course this is a 'fallacy', as Wimsatt and Beardsley would say. The telepathic divination of someone's meanings is impossible. (Though the dream of telepathic communication is one that much literature seems to foster. See on this subject Nicholas Royle's excellent *Literature and Telepathy*, 1991). And there are moments when Conrad's story invites scepticism about the intuitive, telepathic communication of meaning too. Once Leggatt has confessed, very briefly, and without explaining the circumstances, that he has killed a man, the captain responds with an immediate interpretation of his motivations: ' "Fit of temper," I suggested confidently' (181). And Leggatt, who 'nods imperceptibly' at this, does indeed go on obligingly to give an account of a rage so overpowering that it has left him unconscious of the act of murder itself (182). But we are left wondering how far we as readers should go along with this. The captain might well be projecting his own feelings onto Leggatt and misreading him in their light. Just as in the letters Conrad seized on Galsworthy's and Garnett's flattering readings of his story and endorsed them, so here Leggatt might be said to go along with the captain's flattering 'reading' of his character and to respond to it accordingly. We can either interpret the shipboard scene as a beautiful moment of secret and intuitive sharing, or as a more devious game in which Leggatt reads the captain like a book, and shapes his tale to suit his listener. A sympathetic and a sceptical reading of the scene are both possible. And we might suggest that both these ways of reading are necessary to us as literary critics. We need to succumb to a text and immerse ourselves in it. But we also need to pull back and view more sceptically the designs it might have on us.

## Paul de Man: reading and interpretation

The two ways of reading the scene of intuitive communication between Leggatt and the captain open up further issues, which can help us refine our 'what's it mean?' question. Since Conrad is not just presenting us with an interpretative dilemma, but also showing an *act* of interpretation, the problem of meaning is doubled up here. And this makes it hard to know how to read Conrad's 'allegory of reading'. Even if we think that it demands to be read sceptically, to seize on that *as* its meaning is to assume, like the captain, that we have intuited what Conrad means. Conversely, to take the captain at his word, and to go along with the idea that he has immediately apprehended what Leggatt means, is to betray the other way in which we might read Conrad's writing of this scene. Borrowing some words from Paul de Man, author of *Allegories of Reading* (1975), we might say that 'The Secret Sharer' 'can quite literally be called "unreadable" in that it leads to a set of assertions that radically exclude each other' (245).

De Man is explicitly talking about reading Rousseau here, but his comments apply to our own reading dilemma, and also to the question of how we are supposed to interpret 'allegories of reading' in other literary texts. There seem to be moments when a text makes contradictory demands on us, what it is saying working against what it is doing and *vice versa*. De Man goes on to conclude that 'the impossibility of reading should not be taken too lightly' (245). Reading can place us in a bind, in which to be faithful to one aspect of a text is to betray another.

De Man's patient exploration of the kinds of bind in which reading sometimes leaves us can help us think further about what we mean by 'meaning'. He invites us to distinguish between reading – the impossible tarrying with contradictory injunctions about *how* to read – and interpretation. Whereas interpretation wants to arrive at the safe harbour of a final meaning, reading remains – pleasurably or stormily – at sea. To interpret the story is to move from the words on the page towards an account which makes sense of their larger import. Reading, on the other hand, repeatedly returns to the inadequacy of a single interpretation, when faced with all the other things those words might also mean. As we interpret, we may well betray aspects of our *reading*. And this is something always to be borne in mind when we read and offer interpretations of a piece of writing. In the next section of this chapter, we will turn to the question of how meanings are *made*, in order to think more about why meaning, reading and interpretation might present us with almost 'impossible' challenges.

## Saussure and structuralism: the making of meaning

At the start of the twentieth century questions about how meanings are made were explored in a series of lectures by a Swiss linguist Ferdinand de Saussure which were posthumously transcribed and published as the *Course in General Linguistics*. This bland-sounding title covers over the truly radical nature of Saussure's intervention into thinking about how language makes meaning. His major insight was to understand language not as a collection of individual words but as a network of meanings in which one element gains its significance through its relationships to, and differences from, other elements.

We can use 'The Secret Sharer' to gloss these ideas. At its start, the narrator observes along the shore 'a mysterious system of half-submerged bamboo fences, incomprehensible in its division of the domain of tropical fishes' (173). For Saussure, language is such a system – mysterious and without intrinsic meaning of its own, it generates significance through dividing up the world, making its oceanic vastness graspable through sharing it out into a series of 'signifiers', each one meaning something because it is itself similar to but different from another one. '[J]ust as chess is based entirely on the combinations afforded by the various pieces, so too a language has the character of a system based entirely on the contrasts between its concrete units,' Saussure clarifies (1983, 105). The 'concrete units' of a language are phonemes, the smallest elements of sound in a language. Put together in particular orders, they give us signifiers – the sound-patterns which, when heard, conjure meanings for us – the signifieds of these signifers. Locked together by a 'mysterious system' – the tacit rules we subscribe to as speakers of a particular language – the network of similarities and differences between signifiers and that between signifieds, divide up the 'domain' of our world so as to make it comprehensible to us.

Whereas the word 'meaning', as we have seen, connotes inwardness, Saussure implies that in linguistic terms there are no deeps or insides from which meaning emerges. There *is* no 'secret' – nothing hidden away. Language, rather, is divided into 'shares' and significance is a surface matter, resulting from the way these shares are pieced out, and from the fact that each depends on its relation to others. To read following Saussure is therefore not to dive for meaning, but to chart out the paths and patterns which create meaning.

Theorists and critics who followed on from Saussure took up the idea that language's meanings emerged through relationship, difference and structure, and applied this to other meaningful structures, such as social codes or works of literature. Such theorists were known, for obvious reasons, as structuralists. They include Tzetzan Todorov and Gerard Genette, both theorists who tried, in different ways, to account for the general 'rules' which structure narratives. Structuralist analysis can also focus more closely on the rules which govern the arrangement of a single literary work.

The Conrad scholar Cedric Watts, in an article called 'The mirror-tale: an ethico-structural analysis of Conrad's "The Secret Sharer" ', offers just such a structuralist reading of our story, albeit with reservations. In the article, he suggests that this story, 'of all Conrad's works, is probably the one most open to – and most vulnerable by – structuralist approaches' (Watts 1977, 25). His aim – helpfully for our purposes – is to test how far a reading of the meanings of 'The Secret Sharer' in terms of its *structures* might help us to understand it.

Watts begins by showing what a structuralist analysis might look like, isolating 'certain static or synchronic patterns' in the tale, and drawing up a 'structural table' of them (29). He identifies, then, the governing network or structure of differences and relationships, which generate the story's meanings. He does this by bringing to the fore the system of comparisons and contrasts which operate in Conrad's story. The Captain and Leggatt are both young, both from the same training ship (they are 'Conway boy[s]' (181), one of the things that gives them a mutual sympathy), and both alienated from, and distrusted by, their crews. On the other hand Leggatt kills one man, whereas the captain tries to save one man's life (Leggatt's). And Leggatt kills the man, a panicking sailor, in order to avert the shipwreck that would ensue if his panic were to continue; whereas the captain saves Leggatt's life at the risk of shipwreck and the death of his entire crew. The story makes many of its meanings, then, through this patterning of similarities and differences. And it is such underlying patterns that structuralist critics identify and describe when they read literary works.

# Problems with structuralism

A 'structuralist' analysis of the story shows us something of how the story's significations are produced, different aspects aligned with and pitted against one another. The structuralist approach can disclose both elements of the author's craft and correspondences we haven't before noticed within the tale. But, as Watts makes clear in his article this way of tackling a text is utterly untrue to our experience of reading it. As we read Conrad's story we do not see its patterns laid out as on a 'table'. We are plunged from the first into uncertainties, mysteries and doubts – some of which are resolved as we continue to read. We can see this from the start. 'On my right hand there were lines of fishing-stakes ...' the story begins (173). As we commence our reading questions arise which further reading may or may not answer. Who is the speaker? Where is s/he? Is fishing going to be at stake in the story, or is that a red herring? Reading is a *process* in which some answers are given, only to give way to more questions. As Watts puts it: 'Structuralism often tends to halt the kinesis of a narrative by freezing diachronic tensions into a synchronic pattern' (31). Those words 'synchronic' and 'diachronic' refer to two different ways of thinking about meaning. A 'synchronic' approach looks at meaning as though it were all present at once, and could be laid out on a table. Structuralists explore texts as synchronic entities. A 'diachronic' approach, on the other hand, thinks of meaning as emerging over time. What Watts suggests, then, is that a structuralist reading, by fixing a text into a solid structure, ignores the temporal element of reading and writing. Reading is a *kinetic* business, always moving on.

To ignore the process of reading is to miss important aspects of the way a piece of writing might work on us, as its meanings unfold over time. In the case of 'The Secret Sharer', one of the most important things a 'structuralist' reading shuts down are the *ethical* dilemmas it poses. It is all very well to set up similarities and differences between Leggatt and the captain: but how do we know which of the two we are to value? Does Conrad, or the structure of signifiers which orders the story, ever let us know whether it is better to kill one man to save many, or save a friend by endangering the lives of many others? It is precisely the tension of these ethical questions which the story causes the reader to experience. We have seen already, as we read the initial encounter between Leggatt and the captain, how we are pinned between two possible interpretations, needing to choose one, but wanting to cleave to both. It is this kind of reading experience that a 'structuralist' account of meaning can't grasp. To stand outside a text and look at it as though it has a neutral structure is to ignore once again the fact that we have to read it, and that reading itself offers no firm ground on which to stand. Choices always have to be made as we read. And various factors are therefore nudging us towards considering the place of the reader within the production of meaning or signification.

## Roland Barthes: the death of the author and the birth of the reader

Reading, we have said, is an experience which does not give us every meaning together on a table. And decisions have to be made in order to establish which aspects of a work are the significant ones in the first place. The theorist Roland Barthes, who inherited many ideas from the structuralists, and then went on inventively to transform them, took up some of these considerations about the role of reading. In an article whose oracular title, 'The Death of the Author' (1967), has taken on a life of its own, Barthes agrees with the structuralist assumption that meaning is not the private property of an author but is the product of relationships between signifiers. Writers can *only* write in a language that precedes them and is outside them. An author can pick aspects of the mesh of resemblances and differences which generate meaning in any language, but s/he can't simply make words mean whatever s/he wants. Meaning is precisely made possible by the language that is already there.

These 'structuralist' ideas lead Barthes to a different conclusion from that proposed by the structuralists themselves. He suggests that interpretation is a *process*, in which we move from meaning to meaning, never absolutely coming into the safe harbour of what is called a 'final signified'. He puts it thus:

> In the multiplicity of writing, everything is to be *disentangled*, nothing *deciphered*; the structure can be followed, 'run' (like the thread of a stocking) at every point and at every level. (Barthes 1977, 147)

Just as we can follow and lengthen the run in a pair of tights, each stitch giving way to the next one in an ever-extending ladder with no absolute terminus unless it be our toe, so for Barthes we follow chains of signification, moving always onwards while never arriving at a single answer. His reference to the 'multiplicity' of writing suggests an infolded mass of threads. And indeed it is out of this metaphor that 'text' has come to the fore as an important term in literary theory and the criticism indebted to it. The word's origins, from the Latin 'texere', to weave, suggest exactly the interwoven-ness Barthes describes, and distinguish it from the more finished notion of a 'work'.

For Barthes, texts are fabrics woven from larger social, linguistic, literary, and narratological 'codes', on a variety of which any single work of literature will draw, without our ordinarily being aware of it. The task for the reader is therefore to tease out the different 'codes' at work in a piece of writing.

We can clarify this again through reading 'The Secret Sharer'. Leggatt, telling his story to the captain, begins: 'It happened while we were setting a reefed foresail, at dusk. Reefed foresail! You understand the sort of weather' (182). If we don't already have a sense of what a 'reefed foresail' means, in the context of the codes of shipboard life and all the other things one might do with a foresail or other kinds of sail, we will not at all 'understand the sort of weather'.

Similarly, following Barthes (see Barthes 1990), we can suggest that the story itself is structured out of a number of different codes, which we as readers have to identify and disentangle. The very name Leggatt, for example, draws on at least two. The first is what Barthes calls the 'social code'. By calling him only by his surname, without a title, the narrator suggests – using a male, middle-class, public school educated, early-twentieth-century British segment of the social code – an intimacy with him. This usage is distinguished at once from the way the captain addresses his crew, by their roles (chief mate, steward and so on) and how he designates the captain of the *Sephora*, 'Captain Archbold' (194). Here the use of the honorific conveys the greater distance between the two men. Analysis of the deployment of elements of the contemporary social code reveals an irony – that our captain feels closer to an ostensible subordinate, not to mention murderer, than to his official peer.

Employing Barthes' distinction between different kinds of code, we might also read the name 'Leggatt' as a signifier within the 'symbolic code' – that set of signifiers which suggest a meaning beyond the overt one. The name seems to symbolize something. 'Leggatt' sounds like the word 'legate' which means a delegate, an agent or a go-between. This meaning of his name ties in with our sense that he does *represent* something – though we are never quite sure what. The 'symbolic code' is that aspect of a text which prompts us to look for its more secret meanings.

## Testing Barthes' ideas

That we can range so far from the starting point of a single name shows at once the interest and the difficulty of Barthes' approach to reading. Every element of 'The Secret Sharer' could be read in this way. We could follow innumerable different codes out of this interwoven text, looking at how it uses narrative codes, the generic conventions of the short story, the literary-historical convention of the double (with which the captain seems so familiar that he calls Leggatt his 'double' with a surprising alacrity and *lack* of surprise), the language of the bible, ethical codes, and so on.

Barthes argues that it is up to the *reader* to disentangle the threads of a text, unravelling its significations in different directions. He ends his 'The Death of the Author' by heralding the 'birth of the reader' (148). This proclamation itself needs reading. Barthes makes clear that he is not talking about an actual empirical reader. The 'reader' he redescribes is 'without history, biography, psychology' and is imagined as a *space*, rather than a person: 'the space on which all the quotations that make up a writing are inscribed without any of them being lost' (148). It is not the case, then, as people frequently think, that Barthes is proposing an anything-goes way of reading in which I can make up a text's meanings as I like. His 'reader' is simply the imagined 'destination' of all a text's possible meanings rather than its authorial 'origin'. Following the threads and unravelling the codes of a text is a process which I must undertake based on what is there before me. But in the triumphal close of his essay he therefore postulates an impossible 'space', which no actual reader either inhabits or is. An actual reader is someone located in a particular place and time, with her own reading behind her, and her own proclivities and biases too. And no actual reader would ever have the time to follow all the different 'codes' out of a single text.

The conclusion of Barthes' 'The Death of the Author' passes over the actuality of reading in favour of an ideal, structural model of it. It thereby represses the fact that we will always choose some 'threads' to follow, at the expense of others. Just as the captain faces ethical choices, so we do too, compelled as we read always to sacrifice one possible set of significations as we pursue others. Furthermore, Barthes reneges on his own best insights. For if signifiers do point to other, absent, signifiers, then it follows that a text is a force-field which itself pushes some meanings to the fore by excluding others from its terrain. As readers, too, we experience this force. We can see it in 'The Secret Sharer'. It's not just that we don't have the time to pursue all its significations, but that some of them are incompatible with others. Is Leggatt a saint or a sinner? Is the captain a hero or an irresponsible fool? Even an 'ideal' reader could not hold together these all the answers to this question simultaneously. Some readings forcefully knock others out.

# Jacques Derrida: force and signification

This sense of a text as a force-field rather than as a simple fabric is perhaps why we still intuitively talk about an author's 'intention', even if we have read Wimsatt and Beardsley and understand that this is a 'fallacy'. Derrida has suggested, in an essay called 'Force and Signification', that we must find a more dynamic, forceful model of meaning and reading, which can offer a 'conceptualization not only of direction but of power, not only the *in* but the *tension* of intentionality' (Derrida 2001, 32). We can't find a single 'intention' with-*in* a work, but we can register the *tensions* out of which its meanings emerge. Meaning is not just a question of patterns, structures and lines of direction which can be 'traced', but something that emerges out of a tussle, and can arraign us or sweep us up with its force.

Writing, too, can be felt as such a struggle, as Conrad testifies frequently and eloquently in his letters. Compare Barthes' blithe assertion that an author 'ought at least to know that the inner 'thing' he thinks to 'translate' is itself only a ready-formed dictionary' (Barthes 1977, 146), with Conrad's impassioned epistolary groans about the 'hard, atrocious, agonizing' work of writing (Conrad 1983–2007, 3, 327). As I write I am assailed by a sea of possible signifiers which tug me in different directions, or take over my brain, 'all possible meanings push[ing] each other, preventing each other's emergence', to quote Derrida once more (2001, 8). On the other hand, this dynamic aspect of meaning can have its upside. We can see words 'provoking each other too, unforeseeably and as if despite oneself' (Derrida 2001, 8). It is such moments which prompt a writer to exclaim, after the fact, 'Luck my boy. Pure luck [...] I repeat: mere luck'. But when we *read* they also furnish us with moments which forcefully summon us to do justice both to what a text or author seems to want to say, and to those elements which are in tension with that intention and seem to carry it off by main force.

# Wolfgang Iser: moving with a text

How then to do justice to these more forceful, dynamic, or kinetic aspects of meaning-making? These are questions addressed by a group of theorists working in Germany and America in the mid-twentieth century, and known as reception theorists and reader response theorists. Their concern is with the *dynamics* of meaning making, as it happens in acts of reading and interpretation. They attempt to give a fleshed-out story of how it is that, as we read, we move towards a sense of a text's meaning.

One such theorist, Wolfgang Iser, suggests that a text operates through a kind of gentle and seductive coercion, making us into the reader it wants. '[The reader] is drawn into the events and made to supply what is meant from what is not said', he writes (Iser 1995, 24). We might remember the way in which our captain 'needed no more' than the 'brusque, disconnected sentences' in which Leggatt recounts his tale, in order to understand its whole meaning.

How does this work for our own reading of the story? As readers too, we join the dots. Look at the following passage, which ensues after Leggatt has confessed his crime:

'A pretty thing to have to own up to for a Conway boy,' murmured my double, distinctly.

'You're a Conway boy?'

'I am,' he said, as if startled. Then, slowly... 'Perhaps you too –'

It was so; but being a couple of years older I had left before he joined. After a quick exchange of dates a silence fell [...] (181)

A certain understanding of 'social codes' is perhaps necessary to follow this exchange, though we do not need to know that 'Conway' is a training ship in order to comprehend it. But the process of interpreting it is less to do with moving out into questions of British introduction rituals or education structures, than in looking at what is happening between these terse sentences. There is a literal ellipsis of course – we must fill in 'went to Conway'. But more than that we must intuit that the establishment of a common background forges a silent connection between the two men. We 'need no more' than this snatch of conversation to see this. We pick up where Conrad left off, silent partner of the meaning-making process. The text guides us, as we read from one short sentence to the next, to bridge its gaps in a particular way, and to understand that in this brusque exchange, in which the *characters* actually impart very little information, a friendship is born.

## Hans-Georg Gadamer and the hermeneutic circle

To understand 'The Secret Sharer' as simply nudging us in a particular direction does rather suggest that we come to our reading with no ideas of our own however. And that seems unlikely. It may be that we have read other stories by Conrad, for example, and therefore have a notion of what to find in this one. Or, we have read other short stories, and expect this one to have a 'twist in the tale' or a secret which will be revealed at the last minute. More generally, as we discussed in the previous chapter, we come to the work with expectations of what literature might give us – amongst them, perhaps, the hope that it will deliver a meaning. As we read, engaging with the nitty-gritty of the story, there is initially a tug-of-war between our expectations and what the text seems actually to be offering us. We are not quite the blank slate that Wolfgang Iser imagines.

Theorists of interpretation who focus on what is called hermeneutics, take up this idea that we always come to a piece of writing with a bias. They argue that the initial tension between what we want of a text and what it gives us, resolves into an on-going reciprocal cycle. This is often referred to as the 'hermeneutic circle' by theorists such as Hans-Georg Gadamer (Gadamer 1995). Our first expectations will be modified by what we learn, so that our over-arching sense of the story changes. And that over-arching sense will be brought to the next aspect of the story, which might confirm or modify it. As the reader Charlie Louth has put it, 'a reading must continually revise the positions it adopts as it progresses' (Louth 1998, 168). This movement, from a whole overview and initial 'position' to an engagement with a text's parts, which modifies the big picture again, as well as our position in relation to it, is the hermeneutic circle.

In the case of 'The Secret Sharer', for example, we start with the title. In a general way, we understand that this is to be a story about secrets. This jibes with our sense that a short story tends to disclose a secret to us. We approach the story with that expectation. Then we plunge into it. 'On my right hand', it begins. Our prior reading of literature means that we understand this voice to be the narrator of the story. We wonder, then, whether this voice is that of 'The Secret Sharer'. We read on in order to confirm or disprove that sense. And so on. As we proceed, we reach a fuller understanding of what the story *means* by 'secrets' – that the secret, in this case, can refer to unknown aspects of ourselves, as well as to the specific secret of having committed a murder, for example. The story, by carrying us along, makes use of our initial assumptions, and prompts us to refine them.

This flexible approach to 'reading' is specifically endorsed in 'The Secret Sharer' itself. The stolid, unbending intellect of chief mate, prone to exclaiming 'Bless my soul' (175), and worrying away at tiny events which puzzle him until he has accounted for them, is negatively contrasted with the captain's own capacity to adapt to surprises, and modify his behaviour and (quite literally) his course accordingly.

But as we have already seen, it is also possible to read 'The Secret Sharer' as criticizing *too* flexible an approach to interpretation. The captain could always been seen as a dupe, taken advantage of by the absconding Leggatt, and caught up in the latter's plot in contravention of his own responsibilities. The 'calm and resolute' voice of the swimmer who hails him late at night from the sea is enough to 'induce […] a corresponding state' of 'self-possession' in *him* too (179). Other people taking the night watch might be rather more alert than this to a swimmer emerging from nowhere. To read the story faithfully in *this* way – keeping a distance from Leggatt's own interpretations of events – therefore demands that we aren't, ourselves duped, and that to some extent we resist being caught up in its cycle or circle of meanings.

We might want to draw attention here, then, to some of the problems with a hermeneutic approach to interpreting a text. Such an approach suggests that we adopt a position of extreme, and generous, subservience towards it: that we become caught up in its process and succumb to it. Such a surrender may well be a necessary part of reading. But to surrender too absolutely perhaps carries certain risks. After all, *too* faithful a reading of a story would simply be a doubling *of* it – a fact also uncannily registered in 'The Secret Sharer' itself, when the captain swiftly reads Leggatt *as* his double, and immediately takes on the latter's law-defying bravado. Conversely, completely to betray the story would be equally and oppositely meaningless – we would simply have written our own story, rather than offering a reading of the one before us. This position once again seems to leave us with the 'impossibility' of reading described by Paul de Man. And we remember that de Man said that this impossibility 'should not be taken too lightly' (1979, 245).

# Deconstruction and the ethics of reading

Theorists writing after de Man and his friend and colleague Derrida, take up this warning as a prompt to think about the *ethics* of reading. Geoffrey Bennington, for example, sums up well the ethical exigencies we encounter as we read:

> Texts appeal to reading, *cry out for reading,* and not just for any reading, but leave open an essential latitude or freedom which just is what constitutes reading *as* reading rather than as passive decipherment. There would be no practice, and no institutions of reading, without this opening, and without the *remaining* open of this opening. (Hermeneutics is the dream of closing that opening.) [...] It follows that reading has a duty to respect not only the text's 'wishes' (the reading of itself most obviously programmed into itself) but also the opening that opens a margin of freedom with respect to any such wishes. (Bennington 2000, 36)

What Bennington calls for here is a kind of faithful infidelity; a reading which registers rigorously the precise demands a text makes on us, while in its own idiomatic response pointing out that these *are* demands, which could always be refused or taken up otherwise. He thinks about this in terms of freedom. This is not freedom as a free-for-all, but the necessary freedom that reading itself requires if it is to *be* reading in any meaningful sense. To be coerced – either by a text or by an institution – to read in a particular way or for a particular kind of meaning is no longer to read, but simply to follow a set of rules.

We might gloss the kind of freedom Bennington describes by thinking back to the openness we saw in Conrad's letters to his friends. No letter can ever guarantee a response, but letters are usually written in the hope of one. When he wrote to Garnett, Conrad's tone was jocular and affectionate, summoning, on the basis of the friendship they had, a reply which he nevertheless awaited. That's just how letters (and e-mails) work. We send our missives out into the ether, and hope for a reply. But we might also suggest, following on from what Bennington says, that *all* writing always reaches into the future like this, awaiting in its own continuing liveliness a response, which might, retroactively, change everything. Conrad's 'The Secret Sharer', *as* a written document, awaits a reader's response, but can never absolutely guarantee what that response will be.

Writing does that because, in a different sense, it is made of letters too: not as epistles but letters of the alphabet. It doesn't just harbour a cargo of meanings, but is a set of black marks on a white page, whose continuing existence there is the possibility of all meaning. Theorists such as Bennington, writing in the wake of the work of Jacques Derrida, draw attention as never before to the importance – often glossed over – of the brute fact of writing in the meaning-making process. In his book *Of Grammatology* (1967), Derrida suggests that throughout history thinkers have tended to see writing as a necessary evil. It is viewed as something that carries meanings, but is ultimately disposable, like a wrapper or a shell. Once we've got to the meaning, we can forget about the writing that gives it to us. But Derrida makes us wonder what we'd miss out on if we simply left writing behind. 'The Secret Sharer' can prompt similar reflections. It's fascinated by letters and other signifying marks – the captain's L-shaped room, fishing stakes, the mark of Cain, a hat, 'white on black water'. Let's take the hat, which the captain has planted on Leggatt's head just before he makes his escape from the ship:

> And I watched the hat – the expression of my sudden pity for his mere flesh. It had been meant to save his homeless head from the dangers of the sun. And now – behold – it was saving the ship, by serving me for a mark to help out the ignorance of my strangeness. (214)

The hat has been intended for a practical use. That practical use, as the captain also notes, took on symbolic significance as an expression of pity and affection. The generous gift is not received as such – Leggatt loses it as he swims. But thus cast off, a mere object with neither use nor symbolism, it serves as a mark, meaningless in itself, from which he can take his bearings. His forward-looking gesture of friendship seems to have been rebuffed, but in fact comes back to him in a different guise, still carried by the 'same' material thing.

This too could be read as an 'allegory of reading'. Authors usually have some meaning in mind when they write. Their writing is animated by their intentions and may contain symbolism too. It is shaped by the contexts in which they write, and by the things that language makes it possible to say in the first place. Once they give their writing to the world its fate is no longer in their hands. Its letters may not be received in the spirit intended. But by accepting the gift at all, we, as readers, are in the position of Leggatt, able, through offering an idiomatic yet faithful reading of it, to give it back in a different guise.

That is still, of course, an *interpretation* of a passage from 'The Secret Sharer'. And it perhaps falls into the trap of reading the story *too* faithfully, attempting to find a 'moral' in it at the expense of the amorality it also espouses. What would happened if we stayed with the story's own writing? One of the things we may hear in 'The Secret Sharer', if we are not too quick to hurry to interpret it and to find its 'hidden meaning' is the way that it rustles with alliterative, sibilant Ss. Here are just a few of them:

> saving the ship ... ignorance of my strangeness ... secret sharer ... sleeping suit ... straw slippers ... spiritless sigh ... sham sentiment ... start searching ... ship's side ... side by side ... setting sun ... unsolved secret ... Sunda Straits ... the solemnity of perfect solitude ... with tropical suddenness a swarm of stars came out ...

Alliteration, operating through sameness and difference, might remind us of Saussure's suggestions about how significations are produced. And the way that it depends on words starting in the same place and then diverging, recalls too how reading happens through a faithful/unfaithful response. More generally, alliteration, as one of the governing rhetorical figures in 'The Secret Sharer', can be read in this context of significations as a formal device which doubles up the story's theme of doubling. The sound here serves the sense and this aspect of writing shouldn't be forgotten in our quarrying for hidden meanings or concealed secrets. Meaning is not a secret that can be unwrapped, divesting it of the letters which carry it. Letters are necessary to reading and to meaning. And *these* letters, susurrating like two whispering secret sharers, curled up together like spooning figures in the same sleeping suit, seem to rustle with the promise of secrets still to be disclosed.  On the other hand, in their admonishing 'sh!', they also suggest that there is something necessarily secret and withheld about meaning.  Tempting us onwards in our reading, and yet hushing us too, prompting us to quest for further significances while also stilling us and making us listen, they seem to perform in miniature what reading for meaning is all about.

# 4
# Contextualizing literature

'Now, what I want is, Facts' (Dickens, 2003, 9). Thus begins Dickens's novel *Hard Times* (1854), button-holing us with that emphatic 'now'. Our attention arrested, we start to share the sentiment expressed: a voice hails us out of the blue and we want some facts to help us to place it. Who is speaking to us? What is s/he called and what is s/he like? And when is this 'now' to which we've been summoned? We must read on to find out. Dickens doesn't actually supply any information about the speaker's name, background, character or position until the start of the next chapter, keeping us in want of certain Facts, even as that opening voice continues to insist on their importance.

If it is not the case that 'in this life, we want nothing but Facts' (9) it is nevertheless true that facts are important to us as readers. You might enjoy a novel, poem or play for the information it gives you about the time and place in which it was written. Or conversely, your literary reading might leave you craving such knowledge, and lead you to hunt out other sources which will supply facts about the biographical, social, literary and intellectual contexts from which a text has emerged. But how do we go about garnering these contextual facts? And once we have them, what should we do with them? What does it mean to place a text in its context? Or to read a text in order to find out about its context? These are the questions which will guide us in this chapter, as we interweave readings of *Hard Times* with analyses of a series of different theoretical reflections, beginning with Marx and moving through a number of theorists who read after him, on the relationship between a text and its contexts.

Interweaving will, in fact, be our keynote. The roots of the word 'context' take us back to the Latin *contexere*, meaning to weave together. And *Hard Times* is itself a novel made up of several interwoven strands. It shuttles between the story of Stephen Blackpool – a power-loom weaver in the fictitious town of Coketown, fallen upon 'hard times' and mystified by the 'muddle' of the inequality in wealth and rights between the classes – and that of the Gradgrind children, reared under a strictly regimented, utilitarian system of education based on the repression of imagination and 'fancy' and the acquisition of 'hard facts'. The stories span six years or so, tracing how the repressive and oppressive conditions described at the beginning produce effects which ramify over time. The Gradgrind children grow to a stunted and warped adulthood. Louisa enters a loveless marriage with the blustering bank and factory owner Bounderby, and nearly falls into an adulterous relationship with the languid, dissolute and nihilistic James Harthouse. Her brother Tom is also affected by Harthouse's amoral influence, turning to gambling and then, to pay his debts, bank robbery. Stephen suffers under multiple hardships. He is tied in marriage to a drunken and depraved woman, 'haggard and worn' through toiling at his power-loom – that 'crashing, smashing, tearing piece of mechanism' (71) – and ultimately ostracized by his fellow factory workers for refusing to join the union. As a result of this he is driven out of Coketown to find work elsewhere. Returning only to clear his name of the robbery in which the real culprit, the conscienceless Tom, has implicated him, he falls down an old mine-shaft and dies uttering the 'prayer that aw th' world may on'y coom toogether more, an get a better unner-stan'in o'one another' (264). Through all that is 'dreadful and dree' (263) in *Hard Times* run brighter threads: hope and possibility are emblematized in the licence and play of the circus-folk, who arrange for Tom's flight from the consequences of his crime, and the warm-hearted tenderness of Sissy Jupe, one of their number who is adopted by Gradgrind. It is ultimately through Sissy's presence, and her gentle and mainly silent resistance to the doctrine of fact, that the Gradgrind family is saved from utter ruin, and its patriarch, Mr Gradgrind (whose voice opens the novel), taught the 'wisdom of the Heart' as well as that of 'the Head' (217).

# The contexts of publication and the idea of 'background'

How, then, are these stories themselves interwoven with Dickens's own times? Looking at the context of the novel's publication, we can see that the *word* time seems to have been in the air when he wrote it. *Hard Times* was initially published in his magazine *Household Words* in weekly instalments beginning on 1 April 1854 and concluding on 12 August in the same year. *Household Words* was a journal which Dickens had established in 1850 with the intention of publishing essays, articles, reviews and fiction 'as amusing as possible, but all distinctly and boldly going to what in one's own view ought to be *the spirit of the people and the time*' (Dickens 1965–2001, V, 621: my italics). Once the series had run its course, quadrupling the readership of *Household Words* in the process, he then published it in a single volume, to which he gave the subtitle 'For these Times'. He dedicated the book to the political essayist and historian Thomas Carlyle, author of the essay 'Signs of the Times' (1829).

These 'facts' about the novel's immediate context of publication suggest already that this it is a text multiply bound up with the question of its 'times'. What we want, then, is to find out what characterizes these 'times'. Facts on this subject aren't hard to come by. Many works of criticism contain sections which fill in for us the context of the literature they treat. And our most immediate recourse when we are seeking to contextualize a work of literature is probably to turn to such criticism. But it is worth being alert to the ways in which such factual material is treated, and to what its presentation implies. Look, for example, at the *York Notes Advanced* on *Hard Times* (McEwan 2000), which has a section entitled 'Historical Background'. This contains nuggets of information, pertaining to each of the major plot elements in *Hard Times*. It tells us that 'an article about factory accidents, accusing owners of negligence, was published in *Household Words* in 1854, while the novel was appearing there' (99). Against this background of the industrial revolution and its human consequences, we might then suggest, Dickens portrays the impoverished Stephen Blackpool and his indifferent, braggart master Josiah Bounderby, who refuses to listen to any pleas for better conditions from the 'Hands' responsible for providing him with his wealth. Similarly, we are supplied with the 'Historical Background' to Dickens's treatment of the Gradgrind system of education, presented to us in simple declarative sentences: 'The provision of schooling for all children was not achieved until after the Education Act of 1870, but many new schools were opened in the 1840s and 1850s' (100); and 'Nineteenth-century English society was influenced in many ways by the writings of the utilitarians' (100). Here we see, then, the real-life Historical Background against which Dickens stages the Gradgrind schoolroom, with its lessons devoted to facts and figures, all designed to inculcate a statistical analysis that demonstrates, in good utilitarian fashion, how best to produce the 'greatest happiness of the greatest number'.

But here the ironies of this approach to the text's 'Historical Background' also begin to be felt. For the kind of schooling and research Dickens castigates, with its emphasis on empty abstractions and discrete pellets of data divorced from the complications and involvements of lived experience, seems uncannily like an approach to *Hard Times* which would spell out in bald sentences the essentials of a period's Background. Indeed, many of the facts on which twentieth-century accounts of the industrial revolution are based arise from the very government-commissioned surveys published in 'blue books' which line Mr Gradgrind's study, in which 'the most complicated social questions were cast up, got into exact totals and finally settled' (95). Modern historians read, analyse and give accounts of these facts, weaving them together in ways that allow us to see them in a new light. To convert their readings back into mere 'facts' puts us in a complicated position then. Our desire for the facts of the history 'behind' *Hard Times* manifests the very belief in the value of pure 'fact' which the book itself brings into question. To this extent we are already interwoven with *Hard Times;* implicated in but also tugging against its 'context', as soon as we read.

The notion of a context as a 'background' starts to seem insufficient, and it's worth thinking more about what is implied by this common word. A 'background' initially meant the painted cloth at the back of a stage; as a metaphor it implies that a text's 'historical context' is fixed, distant and objectively viewable – a fabric we can see rather than becoming enmeshed in ourselves. It suggests that 'History' can be uncovered by historians and simply delivered to us, whereas literature, the complex, dynamic, unfolding entity in the foreground, requires interpretation and analysis. This absolute distinction between history and literature seems not unlike Mr Gradgrind's grand opposition between Fact and Fancy. But once again that very fact – that we can use an element from the novel to gloss the situation we encounter when we try to contextualize it – suggests that we need to think more carefully about what a historical context is and how it relates to literature.

# History and ideology: Marx

A text's historical context, we have said, is not simply a background. What, then, is it? We must explore here what we mean by 'history'. In the mid-nineteenth century, this very question was being pondered by Karl Marx, and his writings on the subject have had a profound influence on approaches to contextualizing literature ever since. In his 'The German Ideology' (written circa 1845–6, but – tellingly perhaps – unable to find a publisher until 1932), he claims that 'the real basis of history' had thus far been overlooked or treated as negligible (Marx 1977, 173 ). Historians, Marx suggests, 'share the illusion' (173) of the epoch about which they are writing: they describe a past epoch using the very terms in which it was understood at the time. There are, for Marx, two related, problems with this way of doing 'history'. First, the voices from the past which tend to reach later historians are those with the greatest power. The story of an epoch which prevails is very likely to be that of those who prevail within it (Marx 179), in the same way that Mr Bounderby's bombast and bluster and his oft-repeated charge that the poor expect 'to be fed on turtle soup and venison, with a gold spoon' (72) drown out Stephen's mild and inarticulate attempts to frame a different truth. But second, the voices that emerge from a period tell the story of its governing fiction or 'ideology' – and this is something that at once arises from, and covers over, the genuine historical foundations which produce it.

The concept of ideology is one that many literary theorists and critics have found helpful: it's used not only by 'Marxists' but by feminist and post-colonial theorists amongst others. And following Marx's arguments in 'The German Ideology' can help us to a clearer understanding of this oft-used word. This essay attempts to rethink what history is and how it works, and to account for the real foundations underneath ideological fictions.

Marx takes as his fundamentals 'real individuals, their activity and the material conditions under which they live, both those which they find already existing and those produced by their activity' (160). What really counts are two, interlinked, phenomena. First there are the 'material productive forces', that is to say the resources and tools available to humans at any particular time. And second there are 'relations of production', the distribution of people who own these resources and tools, the people who work with them, and the people who profit from their deployment. The interrelation between these two phenomena changes over time. As big industry develops in the nineteenth century, the gap widens, Marx suggests, between those who do the work, and those who profit from it. Increasingly, 'means of production' *and* the wealth derived from it are concentrated in the hands of a small class, 'the bourgeoisie' who grow rich at the expense of the majority, the 'proletariat'. In the case of *Hard Times* we see a complacent few – such as Bounderby, who is both a bank *and* a factory owner – owning all the resources and profiting from the labour of a nameless multitude, 'the Hands'. 'History', for Marx, is the process of struggle between the Bounderbys and 'the Hands' or 'Men and Masters' to quote the title of one of Dickens's chapters. 'The history of all hitherto existing society is the history of class struggles' (1977, 222), Marx writes memorably in 'The Communist Manifesto' (1848).

These relations of production are, for Marx, the historical bottom line. This is the real matter of history. How, then, does ideology – a fictional rationalization of a social and economic status quo – emerge out of this real history? Marx argues that '[t]he production of ideas, of conceptions, of consciousness, is at first directly *interwoven* with the material activity and the material intercourse of men, the language of real life' (Marx 1977, 164 – my italics). Whatever people consciously think about their lives, their thoughts arise *from* the particular ways in which those lives are lived. But under conditions in which 'thought' has become the province of the leisured few, who as Stephen says are 'put ower' (148) the majority who exist only 'to weave, an to card, an to piece out a livin'' (147), that thought will no longer represent the texture of the whole of life, but rather its own privileged position within it. It will see, and peddle as truth, the pretty picture painted on the audience side of a 'background', but not the knotty, messy, reverse side of the cloth. This wrong-sided version of the truth is what Marx calls ideology.

Another way of putting this is to say that ideology arises out of ignoring fabrication − labouring, making and doing in the world − and taking as Fact only the products, actual but also intellectual, which arise from this labour. And the word 'fact', we might note here, comes from the Latin *factum*, meaning 'things done', but which itself comes from the verb *facere* meaning to make, to create, to affect or to do. A doctrine of 'fact' covers over, ideologically, the ways in which products, things done, arise from processes. It ignores how facts are *made*. And if that is the case, then a simple attention to fact will actually be blind to 'context', in its original, interwoven, sense.

Ideology passes itself off as Fact, but is in fact a bad kind of Fancy or fabrication, a fiction that wants to be taken for truth. Since Dickens in *Hard Times* promotes, in the context of a novel, 'fancy' as a creative antidote to 'fact' we must ask, however, what a *good* kind of fancy might be. Or, to put it in less value-laden terms, we must ask what relation literary 'fabrication' has to the context in which it is produced, and to ideology. Marx himself wrote to Engels warmly of Dickens, and other Victorian writers such as Thackeray, the Brontës and Gaskell, that their 'graphic and eloquent pages have issued to the world more political and social truths than have been uttered by all the professional politicians, publicists, and moralists put together' (Marx 1976, 339). Dickens, for Marx here, is able in his novels to tell 'truths' about his world that other kinds of writers and thinkers can't convey. How, we must ask then, is literature able to tell such 'truths'? And does all literature do this?

# Context and its representation: Lukács

For literary theorists and critics who read and write in the wake of Marx's diverse body of writings – writings which themselves demonstrate an astonishing breadth of literary knowledge and insight – these questions prompt a range of answers. Marx's thought was taken up by the early twentieth-century literary critic and theorist Georg Lukács, a Hungarian who joined the Communist Party in 1918, as a way of discriminating good literature from bad, and as providing a template for the kind of literature that *ought* to be written. For Lukács the best literature gives us a reflection of its context which conveys truthfully the 'relations of production' within the world it describes. He writes that

> The work of art must [...] reflect correctly and in proper proportion all important factors objectively determining the area of life it represents. It must so reflect these that this area of life becomes comprehensible from within and from without, re-experiencable, that it appears as a totality of life. (Lukács 1970, 30)

Note the 'must' repeated twice, and the idea of a 'correct' and 'proper' way of representing the world. This is not a theory of how literature *is* but of how it ought to be. For Lukács, Victorian realist novels provided just such an access to genuine historical reality, and he included Dickens amongst those writers of whom he approved.

In many respects we might see why. As we have said, *Hard Times* does give us a very clear rendition of the unequal relationships between labour and capital, or the proletariat and the bourgeoisie. And it is interesting that the only person in the novel who has any link with the aristocracy is the witchy Mrs Sparsit. She trades on her aristocratic 'connections', but her own decline into a dependent state as house-keeper to the capitalist Bounderby demonstrates the shift that had occurred over the previous few centuries from a late-feudal social structure, to the current state of class relations, in which the aristocracy only existed as a fossilized relic.

The novel also goes some way, especially in its treatment of Bounderby, towards exposing the ideology that sustains the inequalities between labour and capital. Bounderby is a 'man who could never sufficiently vaunt himself a self-made man' (20). He is always telling stories about how he was 'born in a ditch' (21) and abandoned by his mother to the mistreatment of his alcoholic grandmother. It seems as though his rise through a series of positions –'vagabond, labourer, porter clerk, chief manager, smaller partner' (22) – to his current eminence as a factory and bank owner exemplifies the heart-warming moral that even the lowliest can succeed if they work hard enough. This was certainly a popular Victorian idea – and was treated more sympathetically, though not uncritically, in Elizabeth Gaskell's *North and South* (1855), through her characterization of the genuinely 'self-made man' John Thornton. The idea of being able thus to pull oneself up by one's bootstraps was based on the principles of laissez-faire economics – what Stephen calls 'lettin' alone' (149) – the belief that through the self-interested pursuit of economic gain and personal happiness, the prosperity of the nation as a whole would increase. But, as Sissy Jupe says, in response to a question in an economics lesson, 'I couldn't know whether it was a prosperous nation or not, and whether I was in a thriving state or not, unless I knew who had got the money, and whether any of it was mine' (60). Bounderby tells the fable of his extraordinary progress to make more laudable and remarkable his current position – but his more devious aim is to use his own supposed success story to dismiss any claims for better working conditions on the part of his workers, whom he characterizes as lazy, grasping ne'er-do-wells. He implies that if even the lowliest can succeed, as he himself did, then those who remain lowly deserve what they've got. And what this insinuation ignores, of course, is that Bounderby's own (ostensibly) 'self-made' riches are garnered precisely through the ill-paid labours of his workers.

Dickens demonstrates here then that the consoling idea of the possibility of self-betterment for all actually dissembles the real truth, which is that betterment is only possible for a few because it necessarily happens at the expense of the many. The Victorian story of the self-made man functions *ideologically*. It implicitly supports the workings of laissez-faire economics, by covering over the injustices necessary to such an economic system. It is not just that Bounderby is telling a lie about his own personal history, but that such stories, even when true, are perversions of the fundamental truth of class relations. And Dickens's novel, by exposing the workings of Bounderby's lie, might be said thus to demonstrate this *underlying* truth.

Such an interpretation suggests that *Hard Times* is able to render for us the 'totality' of 'relations of production' in the historical moment it depicts. It implies, therefore, that literature has the capacity to take up a position sufficiently outside its context to reflect its totality accurately. And, for Lukács, the best literature quite simply does this. But we might raise several questions here. First, we might wonder (despite Gradgrind's injunction 'never [to] wonder' (53)), what riches such an approach to literature would deprive us of. Since Lukács offers a value judgement, endorsing only the literature which can accurately reflect the 'historical truth', much literature is, according to his theory, second rate or unsuccessful. And second, we might ask whether – and how – literature might be said to simply reflect the totality of the world it describes. Lukács doesn't explores the nature of literary representation itself, simply assuming that a (good) text can 'reflect' its context, whereas we must ask how it can do this. We'll take those questions in turn.

Lukács himself, across his work, focuses mainly on the novel. And even within that, he makes a very clear distinction between the 'dynamic and developmental' properties which he valued in realist fiction and the 'static and sensational' properties he saw in modernist and naturalist fiction (Lukács 1963, 20). Joyce's *Ulysses* for example won't do for Lukács – its foregrounding of style, its preoccupation with subjective and psychological experience and its symbolist view of time and history, all skew actual history. Here we might map Gradgrind's rigid distinction between Fact and Fancy onto Lukács's opposition between truthful, dynamic literature, and ideologically skewed or partial 'sensational' literature. Returning thus to *Hard Times* however, we can see that *it* embraces a range of fictional and fanciful writings, from the realist novels of Defoe, and the socially aware poetry of Goldsmith (both authors whom, to Gradgrind's distress, the workers read in their leisure hours) to fairy stories, the Arabian Nights, the 'silly little jingle, Twinkle, twinkle little star' which 'no little Gradgrind had ever learnt' and the 'idle legend of Peter Piper' (16–17). Dickens employs these more 'silly' and 'idle' forms of literature as ways of conveying the reality of life in Coketown. He describes its illuminated factories as looking – but only from the comfortable distance of the 'express-train' – like 'Fairy palaces' (66), and the schoolmaster who is the Gradgrind children's first memory as a 'dry Ogre'. Not – he continues – 'that they knew, by name or nature, anything about an Ogre' (16). One of the things implied here is that *any* literature can be cut out of its original context and woven into new ones, furnishing a flexible vocabulary with which to break free from the tyranny of present conditions. Lukács's model seems to foreclose literary possibilities which Dickens himself celebrates. If Gradgrind hadn't forbidden us from doing so, we might also 'wonder' here whether simply viewing *Hard Times* – or any other work of literature – as reflecting its 'own' context is not in fact to *deprive* it of some of its power.

If literature, for Dickens, has the power to be woven into new contexts, it remains the case that his own novel carries traces of the context in which it was written. We come to the question here, then, of whether a novel can ever 'reflect' its social world in quite the way that Lukács suggests. Many critics have pointed out that Dickens's representation of the Trades Unionist, Slackbridge, as a ranting rhetorician, seems skewed by his own politics, and untrue to the actuality of union activism as he himself witnessed it in Preston, while he was gathering material for *Hard Times* (Dickens 1854, 553–9). Slackbridge's chief act in the novel is not the organization of the workers, but causing Stephen Blackpool to be ostracized by his comrades for not joining the Union. And by focusing on this, Dickens seems to imply the general wrong-headedness of labour movements. Such a bias seems at odds with other insights in the book. In his criticism of the treatment of the workers by the novel's bourgeoisie, he foregrounds and sends up the way in which they are referred to as 'Hands'. This is a synecdoche, a figure of speech in which the part of something is taken to stand in for the whole. In this case, Dickens points out the power at work in everyday rhetoric: the weavers are reduced to the only body part necessary to their master, the hands that work the loom, all other aspects of their bodies and souls ignored. But it could be said that Dickens's *own* treatment of Slackbridge works in similar 'synecdochic' ways. As the only trades union activist in the book he necessarily stands in for a whole body of men who may well be very different from him. Dickens's representation of him here therefore travesties the bigger contemporary picture.

You might find yourself agreeing with this reading. But the question, then, is whether – and on what grounds – one criticizes Dickens for his representation of Slackbridge. To suggest that this is a flaw in the novel is to imply several things about the relationship between literature and context that we might want to ponder further. First, it suggests that literature *ought* simply and faithfully to represent its context. We have already shown that Dickens suggests other possibilities for it. Second, it raises the question whether literature *can* ever represent the whole context of a world. The 'ideological' dimensions of Dickens's treatment of unionism demonstrates to us that literature might always be to some extent marked by the 'now' from which it starts, in ways that it cannot itself grasp. To read literature in its relationship to its context would in that case be to think about how its representations are always entangled in and interwoven with the contexts it also describes. And third, it suggests that we can't just take a work of literature as 'whole cloth'. One thread of Dickens' story, namely his representation of the impoverished, stifled, 'down-trodden' working classes, tugs against another, his 'unrealistic' depiction of a working class demagogue, who harangues 'the down-trodden operatives of Coketown' (136 and 138) for little other purpose than to stir up trouble.

## Louis Althusser: ideology and interpellation

There are other theorists who read and reread Marx in ways more alert to these – contextually produced – tensions *within* literature. We can mention here Louis Althusser, Pierre Macherey and Etienne Balibar. In an essay called 'Ideology and

State Apparatuses' (1969) Althusser argues that ideology is much more bound up with our lives than classical Marxist theory had suggested. For Althusser, ideology does not simply tell fictions about the underlying facts of social and economic life, but constitutes the whole fabric of human life in ways that we cannot simply cut ourselves out of. He explores the way in which 'the state' exerts power not only in obvious ways – such as the police for example – but through our schooling, the media and every other kind of social institution. And – most radically – he argues that this power is what makes us the human beings that we are: 'subjects' who think we are free to act, to think and to write, but in fact can only do this because we are already sub-jected by ideology. He writes that ideology 'hails or interpellates concrete individuals as concrete subjects' (Althusser 1977, 162). That word 'interpellates' is an anglicization of quite an everyday French word, which means to call out to someone, or to question them (as police do a suspect). Snipped out of its French context and rendered in English, it can provide us with a handy theoretical way of explaining how it is that power works in specific contexts and through the languages and relationships that pertain with them. We might turn again to the orator Slackbridge in *Hard Times* to see an instance of interpellation at work. His speech to the workers begins with and is punctuated by apostrophes (in the sense of a literary summons, usually beginning 'Oh...'):

Oh my friends, the down-trodden operatives of Coketown! Oh my friends and fellow countrymen, the slaves of an iron-handed and grinding despotism! Oh my friends and fellow-sufferers and fellow-workmen, and fellow men! (136)

His repeated address to the men, calling out to them and hailing them as his fellows and as slaves, has the effect of making his listen-ers *into* the band of suffering people he claims to be addressing.

Dickens registers this effect himself. He writes of the people 'submissively resigning' themselves to this orator that the fact 'that every man felt his only hope to be in allying himself to the comrades by whom he was surrounded ... must have been ... plain to any one who chose to see what was there' (138). It is as though they internalize the way in which they are hailed by Slackbridge. His address to them seems to make them *into* a group, and to shape how they think about themselves individually.

For Althusser it is not just bad rhetoric that interpellates us in this way, but all social and cultural structures. Schooling would be one example – indeed for Althusser it is, in capitalist states, the most important one. He writes, that 'the educational apparatus [is] in fact the dominant ideological State apparatus in capitalist social formations' and that the school 'drums into [children] ... a certain amount of "know-how" wrapped in the ruling ideology' (Althusser 1977, 154–5). Dickens makes a similar point in *Hard Times* in his representation of Bitzer, the model pupil of Gradgrind's school, who is so shaped by the utilitarian principles and social theories he has imbibed there that, later, none of Gradgrind's emotional entreaties or financial bribes can dissuade him from his intention of turning Tom Gradgrind over to the police. Speaking the language of his schooling, he says, 'I have gone over the calculations in my mind; and I find that to compound a felony, even on very high terms indeed, would not be as safe and good for me as my improved prospects in the Bank' (277–8). Since we only ever exist in relation to society and culture and are always schooled by these, we can only ever speak the language they teach us, and are therefore always produced by the ideologies they perpetuate. Our most intimate sense of ourselves as human beings is, for Althusser, produced by ideology, and arises from the ideological contexts out of which our lives are woven.

Now, you might find this argument hard to buy. It seems to us that we have a unique identity which exists apart from the social world in which we participate. But in a sense, my inter-pellation of you there demonstrates the point. By saying that you might find Althusser's argument 'hard to buy', I address you as a 'consumer' of arguments. In the same way, capitalist society addresses you as a consumer, offering you a welter of different things you might buy, wear, choose to watch on television and so on. In that way it makes you into a person who thinks you are a free agent who can choose. By the very same token, then, it makes you into a consumer – with little choice about *that*. Like the 'now' at the start of *Hard Times,* ideology button-holes us.

We have been able to illustrate Althusser's radical under-standing of ideology through several instances from *Hard Times.* But that suggests that the novel itself has some privileged relationship to ideology – that it is itself able, at least in part, to reflect on its contexts rather than simply speaking through and out of them. Althusser does not write much about literature himself, but in his 'Letter on Art' (1966) (and art here includes literature) he makes some comments which suggest how he views its relationship to ideology. He says that

> What art makes us *see*, and therefore gives to us in the form of *'seeing', 'perceiving'* and *'feeling'* (which is not the form of *knowing*), is the *ideology* from which it is born, in which it bathes, from which it detaches itself as art, and to which it *alludes.* (Althusser 1977, 204)

Althusser's italicized words make a distinction between the 'seeing' and 'feeling' which literature permits us, and the 'knowing' which it is the business of his form of 'neo-Marxist' criticism to achieve. And he suggests that what literature – and art in general – can do is to make us see the ideological forma-tions it emerges from. By repeating in a new form the ideolog-ical context from which it arises, literature makes that context available to be known and read, even while it doesn't 'know' it itself. Literature, for Althusser then, neither simply reflects its context, nor is simply stitched into it. By cutting out threads of its context and weaving them into a new text, it at once 'detaches' itself from that context, and makes it legible to us.

## Pierre Macherey: tensions in the weave

Pierre Macherey, in *A Theory of Literary Production,* a book published in the same year (1966) as Althusser's letter, makes more explicit how these ideas might be put to work in our readings of literary works – primarily novels. The dual aspect of literature's relationship to its ideological context, at once made out of it but detached from it, leads, he suggests, to a tug, a tension or a conflict within a text. He writes that

> what begs to be explained in the work is not that false simplic-
> ity which derives from the apparent unity of its meaning, but
> the presence of a relation, or an opposition, between elements
> of the exposition or levels of the composition, those disparities
> which point to a conflict of meaning. This conflict is not the
> sign of an imperfection; it reveals the inscription of an *otherness*
> in the work, through which it maintains a relationship with that
> which it is not, that which happens at its margins. (89)

Again we might reach for a weaving metaphor in order to unravel this statement. When we read a literary work it is as though we look at a vivid tapestry, packed with detail, life and a sense of movement. In the case of *Hard Times* its 'loom-wrought folk' (to borrow a phrase from the nineteenth-century socialist, poet, textile designer and weaver William Morris) seem to leap out of the text at us as they go about their lives, working alongside or against one another and also speaking together, in ways that address us too. Stephen's repeated assertion that ''tis a muddle' (68) and the circus-leader Sleary's reminder that 'people muth't be amused' (45) seem like the idiosyncratic locutions of real people, as they urge us to reflect upon the 'condition of England'. But when, as literary critics, we look more closely at the tapestry, we realize of course that it is a web of words, wrought by a writer. Indeed it's hard to forget this in *Hard Times*. The narrative voice, so close to Dickens's own position that we may describe it as his, frequently breaks through the illusion of the story it is weaving, to address us directly. And by thus cutting through the fiction – as his use of absurd metaphors, alliteration and hyberbolic conceits also do – he reminds us of the artifice that it is, and prompts us to explore the threads out of which it is woven. Weaving contains, of course, threads going in different directions – its woof is woven against the length-wise threads of its warp, working against them even while it depends on them. And so it is for Macherey. To read a text in terms of its context is to pay attention not only to its story but to the fabric out of which it is woven, and to espy the tensions, the knots and holes within what wants to present itself as whole. By thus identifying a text's gaps and conflicts, we also see the 'otherness' – the excluded or marginalized elements – which are necessary to its vivid illusions. These are the repressed underside of its fabric, and a result of the ways in which it arises from authorial labour, which works over and reproduces the larger contextual and ideological material from which it wrenches its threads.

We can take this over-wrought metaphor of our own back to *Hard Times* once again. The novel, as we have seen, consists of interwoven strands. And it demonstrates the inter-implication of people, and ideologies, across the class structure. Just as Bounderby's pursuit of the profit motive at all costs affects the conditions of his workers, so Tom's robbery of the bank and the ruse by which he implicates Stephen in it, tarnish the latter's name and bring about his death. Tom's character is shown to be a product of his utilitarian education and its doctrine of self-interest. It is of a piece with the laissez-faire economic ideology which lets Bounderby do pretty much what he likes within his factory. (Though government legislation increasingly intervened in factory conditions over the course of the nineteenth century it was resisted by many industrialists and factory owners, as Bounderby's own railing against his workers' complaints imply). Dickens seems to demonstrate, then, that individuals are originally social beings, whose interests and lives remain entwined, even while the prevailing conditions of production set them at odds with one another. The utilitarian education of the bourgeois Gradgrind children has a direct effect on the lives of a labourer, and is governed by the same ideological principles which reign also in the factory in which he works.

However, when Dickens first explicitly introduces the question of the relationship between the Gradgrinds and the workers in Coketown it is in different terms. Rather than describing an interwoven relationship made of the same ideological fabric, he talks of it in terms of *analogy*. 'Is it possible, I wonder,' he writes, interpellating us with an ironic rhetorical question whose only answer can be yes, 'that there was any analogy between the case of the Coketown population and the case of the little Gradgrinds?' (30) Analogy is a figure of speech which implies a likeness or correspondence between two separate things, rather than their interrelationship from the start. There is, therefore, a tension between the way in which the novel's *narrative* strands interweave, and the *rhetorical mode* in which the narrator presents this to us, as correspondence rather than interdependence. It is as though what he is showing us is denied or rewritten by what he is telling us. This is the kind of contradiction to which Macherey suggests we should be alert. Its consequences here perhaps seem slight, but it opens up a tension which can be felt throughout the book, and leads to a telling gap, or silence, at the novel's conclusion.

The conclusion is mainly presented in terms of the Gradgrind family. Sissy Jupe has effected a reformation of the whole household. It is 'Sissy's doing' that the younger Gradgrind daughter Jane has a 'beaming face' (215), and that Mr Gradgrind learns that there is 'a wisdom of the Heart' as well as a 'wisdom of the Head' (217–18). Dickens's language adopts a different register here, departing from the ironies and darkly fanciful metaphors which have governed much of the novel, and speaking out with a simplicity and pathos borrowed from the tradition of sentimental literature which goes back to the eighteenth century. 'Sentimental' here is a generic rather than a pejorative term: the use of the language of the heart demonstrates precisely that different kinds of language are needed not only to register but to generate different kinds of experience and relationship. This language is shown to have profound effects in the world, too. It is Sissy's love for her adoptive family, and the love her former circus family bear for her, that enables Tom's escape from justice. And it is her simple, direct moral appeal to the cynical Harthouse, which has as its only 'commission' her love for Gradgind's daughter Louisa (225), that persuades him to remove himself from Coketown, and the woman he has – in Victorian terms – nearly ruined.

However there is a tension between the novel's domestic, familial and sexual conclusions – which include the promise of marriage and children for Sissy – and what it has to say about 'the case of the Coketown population'. In fact, it has very little to say. We learn that Stephen's friend Rachel labours on in the factory until she is too old to work, that Gradgrind works on in Parliament, 'making his facts and figures subservient to Faith, Hope and Charity' (286), and that the chastened Louisa Gradgrind tries 'hard to know her humbler fellow-creatures, and to beautify their lives of machinery and reality with those imaginative graces and delights, without which the heart of infancy will wither up' (287). The fact that Louisa's privileged life, which enables her to furnish 'imaginative graces and delights', depends *upon* the labour of her 'humbler fellow-creatures' is glossed over. The 'analogy between the case of the Coketown population and the case of the [no longer] little Gradgrinds' (30) here entirely displaces the story of interwoven relationships, at the moment when that story's threads are being tied together. Whereas, within a family context, the language of feeling changes the very structure and texture of the family itself, not only giving Sissy pride of place over the humbled Gradgrind but changing the whole feeling within the household, in the factory context, its application to the life of the majority is merely a graceful wall-papering over 'lives of machinery and reality'. The response of the factory workers is not described, which leaves them imagined as passive recipients of bounty from above, and the underlying nature of their 'reality' is not shown to change a jot.

Now, this is not to criticize Dickens, as some writers have done, for a failure to solve (a word which has a history to do with loosening and untying) the knotty problems of the industrial revolution or of capitalism. Indeed, as I write in 2009 the effects of both of these continue to be felt, in the environmental and economic crises of our global and late-capitalist 'contexts'. But – following Macherey's arguments – what we can say is that, by exploring the tensions within the fabric of the novel, and the way in which at certain moments its narrative woof is at odds with its rhetorical warp, we can feel inconsistencies within it, which are those of the ideological context in which it and its author are enmeshed. The mis-match between the carefully worked-out 'familial' ending of the story, and the perfunctory industrial conclusion, suggests that Dickens's attempts to solve the problems of capitalist society through an appeal to family feeling are motivated by ideological impulses of which he is unaware. It is up to us, as readers, to decipher them.

Althusser talks about what such a reading might disclose in terms of 'knowledge' and 'science'. He says that art makes us 'see' and 'feel' but that these sensations demand that we 'produce an adequate (scientific) *knowledge* of the processes which produce the 'aesthetic effect' of a work of art' (Althusser 1977, 226). By scientific knowledge, Althusser means a knowledge grounded in the reading of Marx. Indeed at the end of his 'Letter on Art', he writes that in order to reach such knowledge it is necessary 'to spend a long time and pay the greatest attention to the "*basic principles of Marxism*" and not to be in a hurry to "move on to something else"' (Althusser 1977, 227). What he advocates, then, is the patience, slowness and attention of a continued practice of rereading, a thoughtful cherishing of texts from the past, since in some ways they may already be ahead of us. We can't just assume that we already know what Marx is saying to us. And we might say the same, too, of Dickens. There is, perhaps, an assumption in the work of Marxist and post-Marxist theorists, that while Marx can be returned to, literature is there ultimately to be known. But in some ways this denies the experience of reading.

## Reading context's futures: deconstruction and eco-criticism

As we have read *Hard Times* in this chapter, we have become involved in its text and texture. Inconsistencies and tensions are things that have to be felt as well as seen, they pull on us as we get our metaphorical 'hands' dirty, unravelling and re-weaving the text's threads as we produce a reading. Reading is necessary in order to know a context, but it is also what a text calls for and summons. In so far as a text summons us to read it, its 'context' also therefore contains the 'future' *in* its very summons. Peggy Kamuf, a theorist who reads, translates and rereads Derrida, amongst other writers, draws our attention to this 'futural' dimension within a context when she writes:

> A literary work has a historical context, as we call it, but no more or less than any document or artifact produced in the past; but the work, if it is still read and studied when this 'context' will have subsided into the archival compost, has a relation as well to a future, by which it remains always to some extent incomprehensible in any given present. (Kamuf 1997, 164)

Kamuf uses here, in her locution, 'will have subsided', a particular tense called the future anterior, which allows us to discuss to what 'will (turn out to) have been the case'. Theorists who explore the movement Derrida named deconstruction, a simultaneous weaving and unweaving which reading allows us to experience, are particularly attentive to the way in which any present moment, however apparently secure in its context, is in fact a mesh of past, present and future, existing in a tension between its history and the unknown possibilities it opens on to. And Kamuf's point is that, while there is still reading and still literature, what 'will have happened' is never something that can absolutely be known. The weave of context opens onto a future it will never absolutely grasp within its own nets.

*Hard Times*, in its thinking about its times, but also about time itself, can tell us this too. Its opening 'now' summons us to a strange time. When the story was first read, by eager and increasing numbers of subscribers to *Household Words*, that 'now' summoned their attention to the 'times' they shared with Dickens. But when we read it we are strangely interpellated, hailed as Dickens's contemporaries even while we still inhabit the 'now' from which we read. This 'now' weaves together, then, its past and our present, speaking to and summoning a future it doesn't know. Indeed, in *Hard Times*, Dickens talks about time itself as 'that greatest and longest-established Spinner of all' (95). It is a weaver in whose fabric we are all entwined.

The novel's reference to the future at the end includes us too. It describes Louisa looking into the fire and envisaging the futures of a number of the novel's characters. This is Dickens's way of tying up the loose threads of the story. But then there is a final apostrophe and hailing of the reader:

> Dear reader! It rests with you and me, whether in our two fields of action, similar things shall be or not. Let them be! We shall sit with lighter bosoms on the hearth, to see the ashes of our fires turn gray and cold. (288)

Dickens here, in that exhortative 'let them be' reworks the language of the laissez-faire, lettin' be, economics he has savaged throughout the novel. In lieu of social and governmental passivity in the face of the frenzy of industrial and economic striving, he summons us to an active 'letting'. The phrase has a double sense. It suggests a stance towards the future (make these things happen) which also allows for the preservation of what is good in the past (leave them be). In a 'present' in which the coke of Coketown and the developments in industry that it permitted is not simply a residue left behind in its Victorian context, but is here, today, in the increasing pressure of our carbon footprints, Dickens's injunction might be said to speak to our anxious present, and through it into the future. The 'ashes of our fires' in *this* context can no longer be read simply as our individual lives, but in terms of the resources of our world which we burn up with increasing ferocity.

Certain literary theorists and critics, known as eco-critics, have already begun to reread our literary heritage in terms of how it might prompt us to think and feel and act today. One of them, Timothy Clark, writes that 'the "environment," ultimately, means "everything" ' (Clark 2009). He does this in a 'call for papers' – an academic genre which appeals to writers in universities across the globe to send what they are working on now, at this very moment, to be woven together in a periodical. His summons suggests that the question of context is by no means simply a question of the past. Context is another word for environment, and environment, ultimately, means everything. To contextualize literature is not to be a dispassionate spectator, viewing a background. And nor is it simply to spy gaps or tensions in a text, which might take us to a grander truth. Context touches us intimately and opens on to 'everything' in our 'fields of action'. It opens itself to the future, and summons us to read it, now.

# 5

# Literature, psychoanalysis and pleasure

'What do you read for pleasure?' It's a very common question but one which seems at first blush to fend off the kind of reflection we've been undertaking in this book. 'Reading for pleasure' is the reading that doesn't require thought or work. It's the reading in which we get swept along by the onward movement of a plot, or give ourselves over uncritically to an identification with, or attraction towards, a particular character; the reading that melts into our daydreams or fantasy life, so that it becomes, for a while, an extension of our inward and intimate selves. To scrutinize this reading, we often feel, would immediately stop it being pleasurable. And even if we do examine it more thoughtfully, the actual pleasure itself remains hard to account for: we like something because we just do – there's no disputing about taste. I might move towards a greater precision about the qualities of what pleases me but if those qualities don't please you we're no further along. In short, then, pleasure, while a very general aspect of the reading experience, is often also a private or inexplicable one. And because of this, finding out what someone reads for pleasure seems to tell us more about them than it does about the literature they read.

But to say that pleasure is individual and to some extent private is not to preclude all discussion of it. In fact, the link we've just pointed out between what someone likes and what they are like, far from closing things down, can furnish a helpful point of departure for our exploration in this chapter of the ways in which psychoanalytic writings might inform literary criticism. Pleasure and identity are, we have implied, connected in some manner. Let's look at the moment in Annie Proulx's 'Brokeback Mountain' (1997) (the story on which we're going to focus here) when the narrator first introduces the character Ennis del Mar to us, sketching in an account of his appearance as though checking him out. Having described his 'high-arched nose and narrow face', his 'muscular and supple body' and 'uncommonly quick' reflexes, she adds that 'he was farsighted enough to dislike reading anything except Hamley's saddle catalog' (2006, 286). That brief reference to his preferred reading matter conveys facts both physical and temperamental about him. Most obviously we learn that he is literate but has poor eyesight. More importantly we infer that he is keen on horse-riding, this being the one interest strong enough to overcome the discomforts of looking at things at 'close range' (to quote the title of the collection of stories from which Proulx's cowboy tale comes). That what he chooses to read are catalogues, suggests, too, that he's a pragmatist – no exotic romances for Ennis; if he escapes through his reading it is only into an imagined future where he might be able to afford new tackle for his horse. Here, then, still focusing on the single thing we know about Ennis's reading, we start to gain a sense not only of his specific interests but also of his more general character traits. We can go further too. Proulx's slightly awkward-sounding 'farsighted *enough*' – where 'too farsighted' might be expected– makes us wonder whether there are reasons other than physical discomfort why Ennis doesn't much like reading. The phrase suggests a more metaphorical foresight, and nudges us to read on in order to discover why most books aren't as gratifying to Ennis as they are to others.

We'll take that as a cue to sketch in briefly the outlines of 'Brokeback Mountain'. From the dreary present of the story's opening, in which Ennis wakes alone in his shabby trailer, down-and-out yet 'suffused with a sense of pleasure because Jack Twist was in his dream' (283), we're taken back twenty years to the past which the dream conjures and comes from and to the first meeting, in Wyoming in 1963, between the two men. They initially come 'together on paper as herder and camp tender for the same sheep operation north of Signal' (284) and then unite physically, in rumbustious, charged sex as they spend an idyllic summer on the mountain. The story loops around this halcyon centre, its narrative moving forwards through the next twenty years of infrequent, snatched encounters between the two lovers (soon married with children), but with the moments on the mountain returned to as precious memories, and even earlier stories – things about their childhoods they've confided in one another – interwoven into the onward-trudging narrative of their inhibited lives. It is not a story with a happy ending. Jack fantasizes about their living happily-ever-after – 'a little ranch together, little cow and calf operation [...] it'd be some sweet life' – but Ennis checks his dreams – 'We can't. I'm stuck with what I got, caught in my own loop' (300). By way of explanation he recalls being taken by his father, at the age of nine, to see the mutilated and castrated corpse of a man who was known to own a ranch with his male lover. Such, he thinks, would be their fate too – 'Two guys livin together? No', he concludes. And so the two men continue to meet 'once in a while way the hell out in the back a nowhere' (301), until one day a card from Ennis to Jack is returned marked 'deceased'. Jack has died, apparently as a result of an accident, though Ennis believes he was the victim of homophobic violence such as he witnessed in his youth. Either way, he is left to mourn his lover alone, solaced occasionally when his dreams of him – which bookend the story – bring some memory of happiness into his day.

The young Ennis is right, then, to avoid reading much beyond the saddle catalogues. When he first meets Jack, he is himself already engaged to Alma and thus inscribed in the heterosexual 'plots' of marriage, breadwinning and parenthood: he's part of the life-story prescribed for all young men of his age, race, place and class. And his passion, sexually fulfilled but socially forbidden, for another man, means that few newspapers, histories or novels available to this Wyoming cowboy in 1963 are likely to tell any other kind of story, or at least not one with a happy ending. There's nothing that will furnish him with any reflection of his likings other than as perverse and prohibited. If what Ennis likes to read tells us something about what he is like, we can now also suggest that he likes books – or not – because of their likeness *to* him, or, better, because of their capacity to reflect back to him possibilities for his own pleasures and proclivities. We begin to glimpse here a two-way, hard to determine, relationship between liking and likeness: we like things because of who we are – that is to say because of what we are like – but what we are like is already in some ways a question of what we like – to be gay, for example, is to like men.

This close reading of Proulx's fleeting treatment of 'reading for pleasure' in 'Brokeback Mountain' has opened quickly onto a range of big questions to do with the relationships between literature, identity, desire and its gratification. It can prompt us to reflect on what makes a literary character tick; on what we mean when we talk about 'character' in the first place; on how an author cultivates our interest and desire and keeps us reading; on the peculiar pleasures which can be produced by the textures and tensions, awkwardnesses and felicities, rhythms and tones of poetry and prose; and on the age-old but still baffling conundrum as to why we enjoy sad stories and can take pleasure in being moved to tears. This last, Aristotelian, question might also prompt us to ask what we mean, precisely, by pleasure and to explore the curious alloy of feelings that it comprises.

# Freud and the pleasure principle

The twentieth-century thinker whose writings and ideas have proved most fecund for readers addressing this sheaf of interrelated questions has been Sigmund Freud. As Proulx puts it in a review of Edward Hopper's paintings in *The Guardian* (Proulx 2004), 'the twentieth century was the heyday of Jung, Freud and psychoanalysis'. Freud's most fundamental premise, which he cleaves to, questions and tinkers with, but never abandons, from his very earliest work, his 'Project for a Scientific Psychology' (1895), to his last book *Moses and Monotheism* (1938), is that we are, primordially and primitively, pleasure-seeking beings.

What Freud calls the 'primary processes' of the mind, the mind's default settings, 'strive towards gaining pleasure; psychical activity draws back from any event which might arouse unpleasure' (Freud 1995, 302). This is what he names the 'pleasure principle'. It sounds simple. But, if it is indeed the case that we are fundamentally geared up for pleasure rather then pain, then it would seem to follow that all our unhappiness – everything that ruins or prevents our pleasure – comes from outside ourselves. If we are unhappy it is because of the cruel world, bad luck, extrinsic accidents. Jack Twist, in fact, seems to think like this: 'Nothin never come to my hand the right way' he laments (307), seeing himself as a passive victim before a world out to thwart him. But what fascinates Freud intellectually, and troubles him as a therapist, are the multiple ways in which people seem to thwart themselves and to interrupt their own possibilities for pleasure. He offers theories about, and sketches of, the psyche which seek to elaborate the mechanisms by which it strives towards pleasure and the compromises it must make in the process. The psyche, Freud suggests, is motored by a fundamental desire for pleasure, which it achieves by getting rid of the energies that bother it and build up within it, fulfilling the internal urges of hunger or lust, say, or avoiding things outside that threaten or over-stimulate it. But such pleasurable release isn't always immediately attainable, or at least not without risk. Food isn't necessarily to hand when we want it, and it is not always possible or acceptable to have sex.

Freud here introduces a second principle of mental function-ing – the 'reality principle'. It's called the reality principle because it takes account of all the requirements that living in the world places upon us – and in particular the fact that we can't do what we want when we want. The primitive urge to experience immediate pleasure must necessarily be supplemented by a more farsighted caution then, and the reality principle is one of moderation and pragmatism. It says, as Ennis does, that 'if you can't fix it you got a stand it' (301).

Ennis voices the 'reality principle' here in his own recogniz-able, terse but eloquent idiom. And Freud is one of the best readers of idiom there is. In his case studies he reports on his patients' own accounts of their lives, analysing through their conversations with him their behaviour, their particular self-thwarting habits, their dreams and their fantasies. Outlining his psychoanalytic methods, he describes how he listens to his patients with a relaxed, 'free-floating attention', keeping an ear out – rather like a literary critic – for the associations and resonances between different elements of their speech, or aspects of their dreams, and tracing the way these 'ramify and are inter-connected like genealogical trees' (Freud 1953–74, 3, 196–7). By analysing the unique idiom of each patient, he reads them as 'texts' – unravelling the 'interconnected' threads of association which go to make up their mental life, and which disclose the things they find pleasurable and keep returning to, and the things they hate and strive to avoid. What he suggests is that people cleave in a self-protecting way to things that have worked in the past, even when they are no longer necessary. On the basis of this, he also makes larger speculations about the developmental life story of human beings in general, telling a story of character formation which – while its enaction is unique in each case – has certain generalizable way-stations.

This story – often referred to as the Oedipus complex – begins by imagining a baby's earliest experiences. The infant, Freud suggests, initially knows only the 'artless, charmed happiness' (to borrow from Proulx, 310) of its mother's embrace. Its world is safe and nurturing, its needs met almost immediately, to the extent that it 'does not distinguish its mother's organ of nutrition from its own body' (Freud 1995, 22). Its body is muddled up with hers. It feels the pulse of her heartbeat and the swell of her breathing; held against her it hears the hum or crooning of her voice and smells and touches her skin. This timeless time is one of rhythm, feeling, touch, smell and tone, but not of meanings, identities, likenesses or differences. It has been named the 'pre-Oedipal stage' by Otto Rank, a psychoanalyst who split from Freud, but it is hard to name and describe since it refers to a time before language, and prior to the nice differentiations necessary to description. This passage from 'Brokeback Mountain', in which Jack recalls a 'silent embrace' with Ennis, perhaps captures an after-echo of it:

> Ennis's breath came slow and quiet, he hummed, rocked a little in the sparklight and Jack leaned against the steady heartbeat, the vibrations of the humming like faint electricity and, standing, he fell into sleep that was not sleep but something else drowsy and tranced ... (310)

The rise and fall of the cadences – like that 'standing, he fell' – and the gentle prolongation of the sentence in a blissful and comfortable near-endlessness lull us too. As readers we ourselves seem returned to some more primitive and pleasurable state, through this depiction of the two cowboys by the fireside. But there comes a point when this entranced embrace must come to an end, for the adult Jack and for every infant. In Freud's account it is the father who ruptures the mother-and-child circle with his presence and prior claims to the mother's love. The father can be understood to represent more generally the existence of an outside world, which the mother also inhabits, and which the child must now therefore acknowledge. The father therefore interrupts, threatens and prohibits the child's pleasure, making it something to be striven for rather than simply being there. But the child's need for pleasure doesn't go away. As Freud says, the internal impulse towards gratification 'never operates as a force giving a *momentary* impact but always as a *constant* one' (Freud, 1953–74,14,121–2). For the infant, the constant urge is constantly met, whereas once this permanent urge meets an inattentive or only sporadic response, it builds. The child therefore faces the agonizing challenge of channelling its desires into time, eking out pleasure in the interests of civilized, safe and organized existence. There is 'never enough time, never enough' (Proulx, 307) for this child. But it responds to this painful impossibility, Freud suggests, in a number of ways. Initially some of its unfulfilled feelings turn towards the father as anger: a quick route to regain sole possession of its mother and the pleasure she gives would be to obliterate the father. As Freud puts it, 'boys concentrate their sexual wishes upon their mother and develop hostile impulses against their father as being a rival' (Freud 1995, 21). But this anger only incurs further pain. Bad behaviour is threatened with punishment, which sometimes takes the form, actually or metaphorically, of the threat of castration: the threat that the child will be harmed, and what is most precious to it taken away, if it does not rein in its desires.

Here, Freud suggests, things must work differently for boys and girls. For the moment we'll stay with his account of the development of the boy, although you may like to turn to chapter 6, for a discussion of his treatment of femininity. Faced, then, with this further traumatic threat, which is felt like salt in the wound of his initial wrenching away from total immersion in the mother, the little boy develops all sorts of stratagems for gaining satisfaction. For a start, he drives his least acceptable desires underground, where they form the unconscious. Until they are fulfilled, these impulses and wishes don't go away, since a wish, as something that hasn't yet happened, can't, by the same token, be killed off either. The unconscious, Freud says 'is timeless' and its processes 'have no reference to time at all' (Freud 1995, 582). It's like a storehouse of past wishes. And in fact everyone's chief desire – the incestuous wish to exist always blissfully entwined with the mother's body – can never be fulfilled, and so it simply abides, a permanent and primitive urge that will never be satisfied. This desire – the root of all our lusts – is prohibited for two reasons. First, it is unacceptable and indeed taboo in the world, for the very obvious reason that nothing would ever happen in the world if every child remained attached to its mother. Second, it is dangerous to the child's own continued existence as a stable self, since, as a wish to return to that sensuous and erotic time of blissful mother-and-child muddled-up-ness, it is a desire for a complete loss of self.

It is no wonder, we might feel then, that we are caught, like Ennis, in a 'loop'. But it is the way in which we live out this loop that then becomes interesting. Freud suggests that the child strives to regain lost pleasures through the private solaces of daydreaming and fantasizing. Along with this inner faculty of representation and imagination comes the acquisition of language – the public medium for naming and representing what is absent and desired, and also for communicating and building relationships, friendships and societies.

Literature too then, arising out of the imagination and finding expression in language, must be understood to have its origin in the child's initial separation from its mother. And this might be one reason why we find it so pleasurable. But all these civilized products of the Oedipal complex are, by their very nature, just not satisfying enough, since they are at many removes from the unconscious urges they cover over. So, Freud suggests, the unconscious desires we experience also seek more immediate fulfilment, battling through our sensible self-censorship, to emerge as dreams, slips of the tongue or strange behaviours. Here we begin to see why we might deliberately harm our own happiness. Tugging against ourselves, part of us wants to say or do something which would mortify our own conscious selves.

The very existence of an identifiable social self, what we call our character, is also a product of the Oedipus complex. Freud describes how the boy, unable to fully possess his mother, nor to kill his father, seeks instead to emulate his father or others like him, in order to gain someone like his mother. Identity is formed then, through a process of what Freud calls 'identification', a term which Laplanche and Pontalis describe as the 'psychological process whereby the subject assimilates an aspect, property or attribute of the other and is transformed, wholly or partially, after the model the other provides'. They add that 'it is by means of a series of identifications that the personality is constituted and specified' (Laplanche 1983, 205). Here we see a reason why liking and likeness might be so intertwined. In order to get the closest thing to what we'd like, we strive to become like other people. An equal and opposite part of this process is a rejection of unsatisfactory identity models. As Ennis says to Jack, 'I don't want a be like them guys you see around sometimes' (300). The formation of identity is, then, one of accepting some things and rejecting others. The question now is how this process results in such a wide variety of characters in the world, with such various means of acquiring their pleasure. Here, again, we must go back to each individual's particular origins. For the infant becomes an individual, gendered, and with a set of unique properties, through a drama which, while general, will be generated by its particular situation, and will play out depending upon what is on hand to fix upon and cleave to. In our severance from the mother we are all 'cut different like you'd crop a ear or scorch a brand' (Proulx 315) and the nature of this original trauma, 'different' in each case, means we always come into the world on a particular bias, flinching from some things, vectored towards others. The Oedipus complex is general and original, then, but it will always take place in very particular ways. In the case of the threat of castration, how it is internalized will depend to a great extent on how the child is disposed in the world, which will depend in turn on how it has already been nurtured there and the range and possibilities open to it. Psychoanalysing individuals is a process of tracing the particular ways in which they have come to be the people they are, and exploring the reasons for the ways in which they seek, and thwart, their own happiness. Psychoanalysis, we might say, is a reading for pleasure. It is time, then, to read 'Brokeback Mountain' more closely, to see how Freud's writing might help us address the pleasures it discusses and those it causes.

## Character analysis

Psychoanalysis furnishes a rich language with which to talk about and to analyse characters, their natures and their motivations. Freud's own literary criticism, along with that of his contemporaries and those following closely in his wake such as Marie Bonaparte, tended to do this. Thus Freud analyses *Hamlet* in terms of its hero's Oedipal desires, writing that Hamlet 'was faced with the task of taking vengeance on another for the two deeds which are the subject of the Oedipus desires' and that 'before that task his arm was paralysed by his own obscure sense of guilt' (Freud 1995, 38). He also links these character analyses to aspects of Shakespeare's psyche, which he diagnoses through his writings. And Proulx's story seems to lend itself remarkably well to a reading which would 'psychoanalyse' its characters in this way. We'll pursue that reading as far as we can, before pulling back and checking ourselves, in order to suggest what it might overlook or wrongly assume.

Proulx initially introduces Jack and Ennis to us in a few decisive sentences, nailing them with a handful of blunt adjectives apiece, but they nevertheless emerge as vivid and solid human beings, physically real, emotionally complex, different from one another, recognizable and true. We can sum them up as though we are describing friends: Jack is talkative and sometimes mendacious, Ennis more taciturn and resigned. Jack, the wannabe-rodeo rider, is the dreamer and risk-taker, while Ennis is more down-to-earth. Ennis plays things safe, reining in his desires, whereas Jack is carried away by his, sleeping with other men and defending himself angrily when Ennis challenges him about this, saying 'I'm not you. I can't make it on a couple a high-altitude fucks once or twice a year' (309). And herein lies the mystery. Why, given that they grow up in such similar environments and have similarly stern father figures, do they take such different approaches to 'managing' their desires? Is it just that Jack is naturally more libidinous than Ennis? It seems hard to argue that that is the case – Ennis's response to his parting from Jack is visceral and his reaction to his return electrified – 'a hot jolt scalded' him (295). The reason must lie elsewhere then.

Helpfully, we are given a sense of each character's relation to his father, and the outlines of two different responses to the threat of castration. Thus we can suggest that the castration and murder Ennis is made by his father to witness when still a pre-pubescent boy, with its implicit message that what has happened to this man could happen to him, doubles up and reinforces the 'castration anxiety' that propelled him into masculinity in the first place. It is for this reason that it has such a powerful effect on all his subsequent actions. That is not, of course, to deny the actuality of homophobic violence in Wyoming in the 1960s (or indeed, as the much-reported hate murder in Laramie, Wyoming of twenty-one-year-old Matthew Shephard in 1990 attests, beyond). But this single, albeit horrific, sight gains over Ennis the extraordinary power to determine all his subsequent actions because of the fact that it repeats aspects of the trauma through which he acceded to identity and masculinity in the first place. And things we learn about Ennis's childhood make it clear that what defines masculinity in his world is a combination of aggression and taciturnity. Bullied by his brother, he is told by his father to 'take him unawares, don't say nothin to him, make him feel some pain, get out fast' (300). Ennis learns, then, that a man stops being hurt by going on the attack, becoming the aggressor rather than suffering violence, and by keeping silent rather than expressing himself. Proulx suggests that male vulnerability in Ennis's world has always been punished, and that the response to the threat of castration or other violence is a silent stoicism combined with a defensive aggression. Rather than 'fixing' a flawed state of affairs, Ennis 'stands' it. And that verb suggests that the fantasy at work behind Ennis's stoical mantra is that of taking on in his own person the attributes of the phallus whose loss he fears: upright, firm, erect. Indeed Proulx has chosen to give her character a moniker which differs by only one letter from the name of the organ he's keen to hang on to, and whose qualities he embodies. Ennis's stoicism – his standing it, solitary like an island in the sea (the literal translation of his name) – can be read two ways at once then. It is the brave but pained suffering of a lack and the repression of desire, but it is also – symbolically – the displaced fulfilment of desire and the fantasized embodiment of a presence.

Jack Twist's journey into masculinity is different from Ennis's. Unlike Ennis, Jack is forced to realize – as a girl is supposed to do (see chapter 6) – that he lacks something his father has: he has been circumcised. As Ennis recalls the story Jack has told him, 'Jack was dick-clipped and the old man was not; it bothered the son who had discovered the anatomical disconformity during a hard scene' (314). For Freud, circumcision as a ritual recalls primitive castration rites. Both Ennis and Jack, then, recount formative experiences in which they are forced to confront the possibility of castration. While Ennis, threatened with castration, hardens *himself* against harsh reality, Jack – figuratively castrated, already lacking – attempts to 'fix' it through his 'half-baked idea[s]', his day-dreams of a 'sweet life' and his fantasies of making a mint as a rodeo rider. He rails against reality when it thwarts him, viewing himself rather plaintively as a passive victim of circumstance. Proulx seems to link his habitual complaints rhetorically with femininity – he's described twice as 'bitching' (287 & 306): we might here recall Freud's theory of 'penis envy', the idea that women are shot through with envy for what they lack. Also feminizing is the physical description of him as carrying 'some weight in the haunch', conferring on him a female roundness very different from the straight lines of Ennis, who is depicted in phallic terms as being as 'lean as a clothes-pole' (304). And, of course, in the only sexual act between the men actually described, Jack is the 'bottom', taking on the same passive role which Alma later plays in her love-making with Ennis. In a variety of ways, then, we might suggest that Jack's sexual and character development is enforced in particular ways by boyhood trauma – the 'hard scene' – that moulds, shapes and 'twists' his character into its adult form.

In fact, Jack seems to present us with a classic Freudian 'case study' of the development of homosexuality. In his overt accounts of the formation of homosexual men, Freud argues that homosexuality arises when the boy refuses to accept paternal authority and instead remains close to his mother, shifting his forbidden desire for her into a desire to be like her, an identification which results in the boy, like his mother, desiring men. In many ways, we could read Jack Twist like this: his mother, when we see her late in the story, is described as gentle and nurturing and she has clearly been close to her son, whereas his 'stud-duck' father is distant and scornful of Jack's life. Jack also seems to have an aggressive relationship with his wife Lureen's father, implying that he remains in the grip of the Oedipus complex, at odds with father-surrogates. But Ennis's life story, as we have seen, is different, even though we have been able to describe it in terms of Freud's more general accounts of the twists and turns of desire and the psychological compensations individuals make.

Here we might use our reading to reflect back on Freud's writings. What emerges is that Freud provides us with the resources to analyse the very specific trajectories of an individual's life and desires, in ways that are sometimes at odds with his own grander theories. And this is a point worth making about psychoanalysis in general – as a theory it itself is tugged in two directions, attempting to set up general 'meta-psychological' models of human nature while simultaneously stopped short – and fascinated – by the variety of human life, a fascination which prompts it to further theoretical speculation.

To sum up then – both Jack and Ennis seem to be legible through a 'Freudian' lens, each bearing the distinctive imprint of his journey through the Oedipus complex. Tracing this journey from the hints and clues we're given allows us to account more fully for their motivations and inhibitions, their desires and fears. It enables us to explain aspects of their characters – Jack's complaining and fantasizing, Ennis's stoicism and occasional aggression – in terms of their histories and contexts. It gives us an angle too on the question of gender. We can see how these two male characters contain complicated mixtures of masculinity and femininity, formed through the different identifications and allegiances engendered by their early histories.

Freud's thought can also help us to understand why this isn't, and can't be, a 'happily-ever-after' story. Reading him alongside

'Brokeback Mountain' brings out Proulx's acute understanding of the relationship between repression, pleasure and pain, and between individuals, their pasts and their environments.

But here, with this mention of Proulx and her craft, we are given pause in our celebration of the possibilities of psycho-analysing literary characters. For we find we have blundered into quite an elementary literary-critical error. We've been treating these characters as real people, talking about them as flesh and blood beings with bodies, memories, dreams, wishes, feelings and pasts, when in fact they are fictional inventions. They have no psyches, they are not in possession of an unconscious. To treat them as though we could simply put them on the Freudian couch is to overlook this. Some of the comments we have already made bring that home quite clearly: Jack's more 'feminine' physique, for example, is clearly not linked to his emotional or psychological development, but is an authorial detail added to support a network of suggestions about his nature, sexuality and identifications. Similarly our remarks about Ennis's name point to Proulx's contrivance – conscious or otherwise – rather than any aspect of his psychological development.

It is a mark of Proulx's art that she has created characters who can cause us to suspend our disbelief in this way, involuntarily almost, revelling pleasurably in a sense of closeness with and affection towards two people who, as we are reminded at the start, only ever '[come] together *on paper*' (300 – my italics). In an interview about the reception of her work, Proulx talks rather scornfully of the 'remedial writers' who identify so strongly with her characters that they send her 'pornish rewrites' of the story, giving them a happy ending. She says these naive readers 'do not understand the original story, they know nothing of copyright infringement – i.e., that the characters Jack Twist and Ennis Del Mar are my intellectual property – and ... [t]hey have not a clue that the original *Brokeback Mountain* was part of a collection of stories about Wyoming exploring mores and myths' (2008). In an odd way, Proulx seems to embody here the 'reality principle'. She is saying that as *readers* we mustn't get carried away. We can't simply identify with a text's characters, reading them as real people. We have to take account of things other than ourselves and our own desires, of the wider world, with its laws, and of the other stories which surround this single one. Indeed her own dry and rather repressive approach to her readers' desirous rewritings resembles nothing so much as Ennis's rejection of Jack's dreams of a better life. Tellingly, she adds that what her disappointed readers 'don't get' is 'the message that if you can't fix it you've got to stand it'. Here, her wish to protect her story from readerly violation leads her to identify that story solely with Ennis, whereas in reading it we have suggested that that 'message' is itself a product of desire and repression and that 'Brokeback Mountain' as a story offers a 'range' of other possibilities.

There are further odd parallels to be drawn between what happens inside the story and how it is read: pointing out that most of the people who write to her begin 'I'm not gay but ...' Proulx implies that they use the story as a cover for their own buried and thwarted desires. And this repeated 'I'm not gay, but ...' refrain, which Proulx here treats dismissively, is in fact very close to Ennis's defensive and self-betraying double-negative 'I'm not no queer' (291). We can see at work in the reception of Proulx's story, then, many of the tangled feelings and psychic phenomena – fantasy and reality, desire, fulfilment and frustration, identity and disavowal – which it itself deals with. This situation can prompt us to two different sorts of reflection: on the one hand we can explore how the very act of reading is itself caught up in desire and repression, and has to do with our own psyches. On the other hand, we can also take Proulx more at her word, and think about how the literary and contextual questions she raises might relate to a 'psychoanalytic' understanding of her story. In what follows we will start with the first reflection, but quickly find it to be linked with the second.

## Reading, identification and desire

The theorist Peter Brooks, in his book *Reading for the Plot,* comes up with a way of thinking about reading for pleasure which takes account of the equivocal nature of pleasure as Freud describes it. Taking Freud's 'meta-psychological' writings as his cue, he explores how narratives work through at once providing us with some pleasure, but on the other hand through deferring and postponing the moment of absolute fulfilment. He talks of 'the motor forces that drive the text forward, of the desires that connect narrative ends and beginnings, and make of the textual middle a highly charged field of force' (Brooks 1984, xiii-xiv). Brooks describes narratives, then, rather as Freud imagines the psyche. For Freud the psyche is as a force-field, in which the drive to fulfilment must be checked in the interests of continued existence, and for Brooks narratives are similarly charged. All the things happening in the middle of them stimulate our interest and hold off the final moment when everything comes together, an equivocal moment because it is pleasurable but also spells the end of our reading. Reading itself then works like Freud's narrative of human development – we move from one thing to another, rather as Jack Twist takes a series of lovers, in order to assuage our urges, but no one thing is satisfying in itself, and finishing a book gives us fulfilment and loss simultaneously. Brooks thinks of 'the arousal that creates the narratable as a condition of tumescence, appetency, ambition, quest' (103) and just as tumescence leads to detumescence, so there is always a come-down after an exciting read. Brooks's account can help us think, then, about literature and pleasure in terms of the structure of a narrative, and the temporal experience of reading it.

How might his psychoanalytic reading of reading jibe with our reading of 'Brokeback Mountain'? Our interest is piqued at the start by Ennis's dream. We want to find out who Jack Twist is and why Ennis misses him. This wish is promptly fulfilled to be replaced by others – we want the characters to come together, and indeed to stay together, but even once we know they won't we continue to want to know what happens to them. And in fact we are given three possible endings. The first comes when Ennis visits Jack's parents, and finds – hidden in the closet – his own old shirt and Jack's hanging up and intertwined. It's a powerful, almost epiphanic moment – the shirts seem to symbolize Jack's enduring love for Ennis, despite his libidinous straying, and the fact that the two will in some ways be forever linked, just as they are by Proulx's story itself. As an image, the shirts effect the kind of fusion which it is the aim of all wishes to seek; they stay together – Ennis sets them up as a sort of shrine – untouched by time or loss. On the other hand, their very timelessness emblematizes that loss: they can only be cherished as a symbol. Proulx's symbol gives us a possible consolation, but then wrenches us back to a more painful reality. It is 'around that time' (317) we are told, that Ennis starts dreaming of Jack. And the dream – the story's second quasi-ending – returns us at once to the beginning of the narrative and, through the memories it conjures up, to the beginning of the events which precipitated it.

In a way, the dream itself could be read as embodying what literature, too, gives us – an ostensibly coherent, condensed and aesthetically pleasing form which conveys at once loss and gratification and which opens up imaginative possibilities beyond its own bounds. Let's read it. Jack is there as Ennis 'had first seen him, curly-headed and smiling', but

> the can of beans with the spoon handle jutting out and balanced on the log was there as well, in a cartoon shape and lurid colors

> that gave the dreams a flavor of comic obscenity. The spoon
> handle was the kind that could be used as a tire iron. (317)

The dream is sad, comic, sexy and violent all at once – rather like Proulx's story in fact. It brings back Jack, but also marks his loss. On the one hand, it makes a castrating tire iron into a phallic spoon, which then recalls the fireside feasts and more erotic spooning that happened during the 'old, cold time on the mountain'. Here, Ennis's deepest and least fulfillable wishes – to regain lost time, to have his lover back – are symbolically fulfiled. On the other hand, the spoon is, simultaneously, a tire iron – and, oddly, this too might be seen to fulfil a different desire on Ennis's part: the wish to be sure that his own life choices have been the correct ones. If a phallic spoon handle can also be an instrument of violence – well then on the one hand Jack was murdered, but on the other Ennis's repressions and renunciations are vindicated, and he has been right to remain in the closet. The dream cuts both ways at once, and it does so through its use of condensation, one of the dream-workings Freud describes, where an image, a person, or even a word, can carry several, sometimes conflicting, meanings simultaneously.

Condensations can be seen at work in literature too, in things like literary symbols or oxymorons. The very name of Brokeback Mountain, for example, at once conjures, through association, the pleasurable peaks that were reached on it, and the broken dreams and bodies which such abandoned pleasures risk. Similarly the title of Proulx's short story collection, *Close Range*, implies a constrained and inhibiting place, close in the sense of claustrophobic, and yet at the same time a range, where there is latitude and scope to roam seemingly at will. In all these ways, pleasure and prohibition are intertwined by Proulx, given and cancelled at the same time, never one without the other. And reading her through Freud's understanding of dreams can help us understand how certain rhetorical aspects of (especially) literary language might give us pleasure precisely through offering us several things at once, fulfiling our desire not to have to eke out our pleasures in time, but giving them to us in an impossible simultaneity.

Ennis's condensed and oxymoronic dream is not the absolute end of the story though. Again our desire is displaced. The very final sentence reads

> There was some open space between what he knew and what he tried to believe, but nothing could be done about it, and if you can't fix it you've got to stand it. (318)

That first clause is quite enigmatic. It refers, I think, to Ennis's wish to believe that Jack was always true to him, alongside his knowledge that he wasn't, that there were other men. Again here we see a disjunction between desire and reality, the tug and the space between the two having to be withstood and inhabited if they can't be connected. Ending things with Ennis's stoical refrain, converted into standard English by the narrative voice which echoes it, could be felt to cut things off repressively, concluding with a simple appeal to the 'reality principle' and leaving us with nothing but a world of woe. But on the other hand, as an echo of Ennis's idiomatic catch-phrase, it also returns us as readers to an earlier moment in the story, giving us a pleasurable jolt of recognition and rekindling our sense of Ennis even as his story ends. Just as Brooks suggests, then, the movement of the narrative is one of desire and its deferral, and this very movement is given us in miniature in each of its three 'endings', which at once satisfy us and leave us wanting.

Narratives, we can see now, work on our desires through working like desire, propelling us onwards, seeking gratification on the way, and occasionally seizing on a particular character, image, thing or word for expression and relief, investing it with a 'brilliant charge' (Proulx, 307) that makes it stand out luminously. Whereas Brooks places his explicit emphasis on narrative and plot, then, what emerges from his analyses and ours is that these demand the resistance of something else, which we might describe in literary-critical terms as the lyrical. Lyrical moments are ones of pure, unfettered expression; they are where writing sings out as though unconstrained, and where time seems to stand still for a moment of pure joy. The critic Susan Stanford Friedman links the lyric mode to the pre-Oedipal state, describing it as 'like the lyric moment. [...] seemingly timeless and unbounded, prelapsarian and Edenic' (Friedman 1989, 165). Alongside the thrust of narrative, with the phallic movement Brooks describes from tumescence to detumescence and back again, there is also, then, a different kind and rhythm of writing, more linked to the primitive relationship to the mother's body than to adult sexuality. And if, in 'Brokeback Mountain', women don't get much of a look-in, Ennis's wife Alma baffled and thwarted by the way his desires are vectored elsewhere, Jack's wife Lureen represented as 'hard' and disdainful, we might suggest that the writing itself nevertheless has space for a relationship to more 'feminine', pre-gendered or perhaps 'queer' qualities.

## Queerness, style and queer theory

Proulx's story is written mainly in a quick prose studded with incisive apothegms, hurrying us along, eliding four missing years between Brokeback Mountain and the men's next meeting, and condensing much of the twenty years thereafter. But it's capable too of a more yielding, expansive dilation, and is punctuated with lyrical moments all the more piercing for the idiomatic, off-kilter quality of their expression. You want to keep quoting Proulx, cherishing and returning to these phrases. Here's a good bit for example: 'Ennis, riding against the wind back to the sheep in the treacherous, drunken light, thought he'd never had such a good time, felt he could paw the white out of the moon' (289). The last clause is unforgettable, I think, conveying the ecstatic, anything's-possible exhilaration of falling in love, contentment and yearning oddly blent, in an image which combines a sublime reaching for the heights with the brute animal energy and slightly clumsy fumbling of that bear-like 'paw'. The beauty of these moments is perhaps not untainted by the pathos of their insufficiency, and nor is it untouched by comedy: if we necessarily idealize the things which stand in for our lost ideal, then at the same time we are obliged to acknowledge their less-than-ideal idiosyncrasies. The curly-headed, smiling, youthful Jack is given the 'twist' of rather unsexy buck-teeth, for example.

Twists, quirks and other queerness are not only what make plots interesting, but literary characters too. Much of the energy, pleasure *and* humour in Proulx's writing lies in her sharp ear for idiom and the ways in which she renders characters through the idiosyncrasies of their speech, as we have seen with Ennis's tersely stated mantra. Like the process of identity formation through identification, which Freud describes in his account of the Oedipus complex, literary characterization itself works through giving characters distinguishable traits, rag-bag assortments of properties and verbal habits which make up recognizable characters, whom we can then quote and love, making aspects of them part of ourselves, identifying with them in turn.

At a larger level this is what makes the writing itself identifiable, too. The story is recognizably Proulx's in style, and bears some of the trade-mark signatures which traverse her work, such as the evocative, funny and non-realistic naming of her characters, which flirt with and hint at meanings which they never unequivocally deliver. Reading literature in the light of Freud's writings, then, can help us understand not only characters, but characterization, and the ways in which an author's style seems to have a character of its own.

These questions of character, quirks, identification and style can help us think in a different way about 'queerness' too. As we have said, Freud's *overt* accounts of the development of male homosexuality are rather restrictive and pathologizing. They tend to imagine homosexuality as a deviation from a straight norm. But his more general understanding of the quirkiness of identification can help us to see that there is something *necessarily* queer about identity and its relationship to desire. Identity can only ever mark itself out through its preferences, biases, twists and inflections.

These ideas have been taken up in the eighties and nineties by queer theorists, such as Eve Sedgwick, Judith Butler and Leo Bersani. These writers draw inspiration not only from Freud, but from the historian and theorist of knowledge and sexuality Michel Foucault. Foucault has suggested, in his three-volume *History of Sexuality*, that the ways in which people *take* their sexual pleasure are not always understood to define their nature or identity in the same ways across history. Indeed, he argues that 'homosexuality' as an *identity* (as distinct from the fact or act of men loving men) is a nineteenth-century invention. For Foucault, it is through the very medical, scientific and legal institutions which seek to treat, know or punish 'the homosexual' that a particular set of traits becomes fixed into 'the homosexual identity' in the first place. Dating this shift to 1870, Foucault argues that 'the sodomite had been a temporary aberration; the homosexual was now a species' (Foucault 1976, 43). Queer theorists draw on these ideas in their readings of literature, to show how the very mechanisms of its delineation of character – according characters identifiable tics and qualities – can enlighten us about the ways in which society itself gathers together *certain* preferences and styles, and fixes them into a supposed identity. Even literature which seems very straitjacketing in its approach to identity can, for these theorists, open up new possibilities, just by showing us the workings of characterization in the first place.

## Language and desire

All of the complicated literary pleasures we have discussed – the character-based, narrative, lyrical, tonal and stylistic features, are, it goes without saying, made possible by the language which delivers them. And language, as we have said, is one of the compensatory pleasures to which the infant accedes when it makes the painful journey out of the Oedipus complex. To some extent, then, language is always marked by loss even as it strives towards pleasure and attainment. Furthermore, language is never something we can simply own. We learn and inherit it from those around us, from our parents and the wider world. It is both ours and not ours and we can never know it fully, since it is that through which we know, speak, spell, sing and write. As we said in chapter 3, it makes its meanings through connections and resonances, which themselves promise and point onwards, while never being fully there in one place. For that reason, the theorist Jacques Lacan, rereading Freud in the light of Saussure's linguistic theories (discussed in chapter 3), has suggested that 'the unconscious is structured like a language' (see Lacan, 1977): it is the desirous underside which propels our conscious selves even as we strive to master it. But if we can't entirely master it, we are nevertheless able to put a spin on it to serve our own wishful ends. We can see this in the way that Jack and Ennis use language in 'Brokeback Mountain'.

Their language and desires seize on the images and lexis they have to hand. 'Gun's going *off*' Jack ejaculates, referring to the necessary equipment of the cattle-herder in order to describe his own. The narrator points out this tendency too, remarking that Ennis dredges 'up a rusty but still useable phrase from the childhood time before his mother died' (310) during his tender fireside embrace with Jack, and that, 'not big on endearments', he calls Jack 'little darlin' (295) as he does his daughters and horses. Language itself, then, embodies the tensions between private pleasure and the reality of the public world which we have traced through this chapter. It has agreed-upon meanings as well as private associations, it can serve us and betray us, and it can deliver clear-sighted rational propositions as well as touching us more primitively, through its rhythms and textures. These things are not at odds but simultaneous. When Proulx writes that 'the ochre-branched willows swayed stiffly, pollened catkins like yellow thumb-prints' (306), the adjectives and the simile touch us through their exquisite precision, even while the syllabically balanced phrase, pivoting round that central caesural comma, moves us more physically and intuitively.

## Contextualizing pleasure and psychoanalysis

We have already pointed out Proulx's own identification with that phrase 'if you can't fix it, you've got to stand it', itself pivoting on a centrally-placed comma. In some ways we might now read Ennis's and Proulx's words as expressing the dilemma of the disciplined writer, striving for idiomatic expression within a language which is never simply her own, withstanding its tugs in one direction and another. There is little doubt that once Proulx has written she is quite jealous of her stories and wants to retain authorial ownership of them. We saw that in her rather defensive response to readerly appropriations of her story, and the way in which she invoked the laws of 'copyright infringement', and the context of 'Brokeback Mountain' within a larger collection of tales, in order to reject its hijacking by hedonistic readers for pleasure. Two further things might be said about this now, by way of conclusion. First, Proulx is right to suggest that a story can never simply be an 'open range [for readers] to explore their own fantasies'; or rather, it can only do this through the partic- ular tensions, openings and constrictions it enacts. On the other hand, her story is only legible at all in so far as it opens itself up in a public language and *to* a public whose own most intimate fantasies will ineluctably inflect and drive their readings. Indeed, were it not repeatable in other contexts and susceptible of other spins and treatments, it could not have been made into an award-winning, profit-making film. Again loss brings profit and vice versa. Second, Proulx's emphasis on the context of the story itself opens things out as much as it closes things in. The admonition that the story must be placed in the context in which it appears is, after all, an incitement to read, enjoy, speculate, understand and fantasize about the other stories in *Close Range*. 'Brokeback Mountain' can be linked with other contexts too. We might wish to place it, for example, within a pastoral tradition, connecting the way in which its two cowboys 'mangle[d] their way through some songs' (290) with the more melodious flutings of shepherds stretching back to Virgil and beyond. Indeed Virgil's second Eclogue itself offers us an idyllic vision of homosexual love, and has been appropriated as a generic model with which to encode queer desires by a range of subsequent readers and writers, throughout the ages – A. E. Housman would be one example. Since 'context' and 'reality' must themselves be read, they are not, themselves, protected from the wishes they seek to repress. Loves that dare not speak their name outright have long found in literature ways to do so obliquely.

Lastly, while we are taking Proulx's repressive admonition to read in context as a spur to further reading pleasures, we might note that one important context in which she writes is that of Freud's writings themselves. 'There is as little chance of going back to pre-Freudian beliefs as there is of going back to pre-Copernican beliefs' as John Forrester has observed (Forrester 1997, 2). Our readings of Proulx's characters in terms of the 'Oedipus complex' is doubtless partly possible because of the fact that she herself is aware of this powerful way of accounting for characters. Freud's writings themselves, then, can never simply be used to master or repress Proulx's writing or anyone else's. In the case of twentieth-century writing they represent, in a sense, its unconscious – what it knows without knowing. And they can also, as we have seen, provide a set of connections, suggestions and hints about the very particular pleasures reading literature is able to prompt.

# 6

# Literature and gender

The simple fact and yet difficult question of sexual difference has engendered literature throughout the ages. From the book of *Genesis* to *Jane Eyre* (1847) and from Chaucer's *The Wife of Bath's Tale* (c. 1387) to Margaret Atwood's *The Handmaid's Tale* (1985), writers have explored the differences between the sexes. In fact it is hard to think of a literary work in which such differences are *not* in some way at issue, as though literature itself is necessarily marked by sex. In this chapter we'll explore the liaisons between literature, sex and gender through reading Christina Rossetti's poem 'Goblin Market' alongside the writings of feminist and gender critics.

Rossetti wrote her jaunty, haunting poem, about two young women facing the wiles and lures of strange 'goblin merchant men' (Rossetti 2001, 1.474), in 1859, a time when women's role in the world was a subject of quite fevered public debate. Sexual differences are age-old, but the language and discussions they generate have complex genealogies. It is important to call this to mind: this is a subject which touches us so primitively that it can be difficult to reflect upon it. We are all sexed beings, chromosomally imprinted from the start, our genetic codes containing 'information' about us before we are ever in a position to know it. Our sex is a given for us. But just as writing has to be read, so the physical facts of sexual difference generate their significances within particular contexts and cultures.

# Feminism in its contexts

'Goblin Market' was written in England at a time when women had just begun to square up in an organized way to the long-standing injustices of a society in which men had privileges and freedoms denied to women. Societies structured in this fashion – in which power and privilege reside ultimately with men – are described as patriarchies. And Victorian Britain, despite the presence of a female monarch, was emphatically patriarchal. Rossetti and her female contemporaries were not only debarred from voting but had no right to a university education or professional training, or even to own property once married. Thinkers such as Barbara Bodichon, John Stuart Mill and Florence Nightingale argued trenchantly that this was unjust. The discussions which surrounded claims for women's equality were known as 'The Woman Question' – a portentous title which in fact concealed multiple questions, and questions which could not help being about men as well as about women: Are women fundamentally different from men not just physically but in terms of character? If there *are* certain characteristics which seem 'masculine' and others which seem 'feminine' do these derive from biological differences or from the way that society treats people of each sex? Either way, *should* men and women be treated differently? Are the rights of woman the same as those of man?

These questions received, and continue to receive, a range of responses. The liberal position – from which the first twentieth-century feminist critics trace their descent – was that gendered differences were cultural rather than natural. The liberal political theorist, John Stuart Mill, ten years after the publication of 'Goblin Market', writes:

> What is now called the nature of women is an eminently artificial thing – the result of forced repression in some directions, unnatural stimulation in others. (Mill 1984, 276)

This position would today be described as *anti-essentialist*. (See chapter 2 for a different discussion of essence and essentialism). Mill, and others like him, argue that the qualities usually thought to be innately feminine are not essentially linked to being female, but are the artificial result of the patriarchal society in which women live, and the laws and social constraints to which they are subject. This argument employs a distinction which many subsequent feminists have found helpful, between biological *sex* and the cultural codes of *gender*. Females, that is to say, are not necessarily feminine. And nineteenth-century liberals argued that femininity was a kind of fiction, written by patriarchal society. Only by according women equal rights to fulfil themselves would it be possible to see who they really were and what they were really capable of.

This vision was partially realized in the fifty years that followed. Feminists won many legal battles against gender inequality, until – in 1928 when the voting age was equalized in Britain – women had most of the same fundamental legal rights as men. But after the Second World War they started to point out that more insidious but no less thwarting forms of constraint remained. Simone de Beauvoir in *The Second Sex* (1949) (published, in fact, only a year after French women had won the vote) and Betty Friedan in *The Feminine Mystique* (1961) both drew attention to the way in which women are shaped and inhibited through patriarchal *ideologies*, which purvey what Beauvoir refers to as 'the myth of woman'.

She writes:

> [H]umanity is male and man defines woman not in herself but as relative to him; she is not regarded as an autonomous being. [...] she is the incidental, the inessential as opposed to the essential. (Beauvoir 1972, 16)

Woman, according to Beauvoir, has always been determined and constructed as 'not-man'. Her gendered attributes are assumed to be her natural properties, but in fact they are projected onto her as a result of male self-definition. In order for man to assert himself as active and dominant, woman must be passive and subservient, in order for man to think of himself as rational, woman must be irrational. These ways of thinking are so insidious and embedded in our history, philosophy, literature and thought-patterns that mere changes to the law will not suffice. The fiction of femininity outlasts factual alterations in the fabric of the state.

These realizations led to feminist activity on a number of fronts – moves to 'raise the consciousness' of women who may themselves have imbibed sexist ideologies, to change the structure of the work-place, improve child-care facilities, address imbalances in pay and so on. But what is crucial for our purposes is that feminists – such as the writers Kate Millet and Germaine Greer – began also to look more closely at the various media through which the myth of femininity was promulgated. They held up diverse works for scrutiny and condemnation. In a chapter of *The Female Eunuch* (1970) called 'The Stereotype', for example, Greer mentions instances from the poetry of Spenser, Shakespeare and Thomas Lodge, the history of Western art, and the magazines *Vogue, Nova* and *Queen*, to demonstrate how the stereotype of the beautiful, objectified and passive woman has emerged through time and across a range of cultural forms. This way of approaching litera-ture, trawling poems, novels and plays for the stereotypes of women they peddled, was taken up in university literature departments, in particular in the United States. As we saw in chapter 4, literature is a place where ideologies can be perpetu-ated, but also exposed. And so the first generation of feminist literary critics found it. It is to their readings that we will first turn.

# Images of women in 'Goblin Market'

Many of the first feminist literary critics examined literature, by men *and* women, in order to identify the positive or negative images of women it conveyed. It would be possible to give a reading of 'Goblin Market' along these lines, arguing that it offers a stultifying representation of femininity, demurely curtseying to nineteenth-century assumptions about gendered identities. Let us test the merits of such an approach. It might go something like this:

'Goblin Market', written by the pious, high-Anglican, mid-Victorian maiden, Christina Rossetti, tells the story of two sisters, Lizzie and Laura. It is a didactic story and a very old one – a version of the fall of Eve in *Genesis*. A focus on its depiction of the two sisters leads us to see that the poem cautions against female curiosity and over-reaching, and advocates obedience, piety and continence. The women Rossetti represents are, initially, two 'modest maidens' (l. 209), who seem – although unmarried – to fulfil exactly the domestic roles prescribed by Victorian patriarchs, placidly cooking, sewing and 'set[ting] to rights the house' (l. 204). Golden-haired and 'neat like bees' (l. 201) they are, in the words of Coventry Patmore's notorious poetic paean to domestic womanhood, 'angels in the house'. But angels can always become fallen angels. Lizzie and Laura, leaving the safety of their proper environment, loiter in the 'mossy glen' (l. 86) and listen to the seductive cries of the goblin men, purveyors of luscious but forbidden fruit. Like Eve, 'curious Laura' (l. 69) ignores the prohibitions placed upon her, daring to defy authority and to indulge her appetite. In a symbolic loss of virginity, she exchanges one of her golden curls for a cornucopia of fruit, on which she gorges greedily: 'she sucked and sucked and sucked the more/Fruits which that unknown orchard bore'(l. 135). Such wanton, noisily physical indulgence violates the requirements of demure femininity and must be punished. Laura, like a typical 'fallen woman', becomes ill and slatternly and wastes away, losing all pleasure in her former maidenly activities. Unable any longer to see or hear the goblin men, she is condemned to hanker after the now-unattainable fruit. She is saved only by an act of sisterly devotion. The angelic Lizzie ventures among the goblin men, who attack her physically, bombarding her with fruit in an attempt to get her to eat. Lizzie does not succumb, but returns, juice-smeared, to her sister, who – tasting the fruit for a second time – is cured. Altruistic love wins the day, and the sisters live happily ever after.

We can round up this account by suggesting that the poem offers nothing but propaganda for domesticity, duty and dullness. Its heroine is an unrealistic blend of exceptional beauty and saintly virtue. Rossetti condemns curiosity, experimentation and desire and suggests that only the most demure, self-sacrific-ing women will thrive. We can use 'Goblin Market', then, to exemplify the ways in which, in the nineteenth century, litera-ture offered women only stereotyped images of themselves. And we can also suggest that literature *ought,* in our enlightened age, to offer more realistic depictions of women as they are, or could be.

That's how the kind of feminist critique of Rossetti's poem which focuses on 'images of women' might go. This sort of approach had its hey-day in the 1960s and 1970s when the feminist movement is said to have entered its 'Second Wave'. Susan Koppelman Cornillon collects together a series of essays employing this method in her influential book *Images of Women in Fiction: Feminist Perspectives* (1972) and introduces them thus:

> The[se] writings [...] enlighten our understanding by helping us distance ourselves from the literature; [they] prevent us from falling into the traps of the implications and prescriptions for behavior, for the limiting self-images and aspirations for women

embodied in much of the literature that we have been taught is important. (Cornillon 1972, ix)

Literature, then, is not to be consumed or enjoyed with abandon, nor even approached too closely. It must be held at a wary and critical distance. The seductive blandishments of generations of authors must be identified for the insidious coercions they are, in order to 'prevent us from falling into ... traps'. We might quote Rossetti's poem here: 'their offers should not charm us/Their evil gifts would harm us' (l. 65–6). Like Laura and Lizzie, feminist critics must identify the harm within literary charm, in order not to fall. And, as the title of Cornillon's book implies, this must be done through scrutinizing literature for the merits and demerits of the 'images of women' it offers. Critics should condemn those which are 'limiting' and offer only 'prescriptions' and narrow stereotypes, and celebrate those which show women that they 'are equal in all respects to men' (Cornillon, x).

It's easy to see the political punch of this way of reading literature. The kind of responses to 'Goblin Market' I outlined are the sort of thing we might find ourselves saying today about idealizing or demonizing images of women on television and in magazines or adverts. They are a way of pointing out that such images are not natural, but carry with them ideological assumptions. In reading literature, too, this approach can bring us up short and make us explore critically the designs it has on us. This type of criticism credits literature with considerable power, implicitly pointing to its continued relevance to us and our lives, through suggesting how we form our ideas of ourselves by taking in the idealized models we encounter as we read.

On the other hand, this approach treats literature's power with great disdain. Paradoxically, it responds to what it perceives as prescriptive literature by being prescriptive itself, ruling some works unsuitable for the feminist cause, and laying down the law as to what good writing ought to do. And underpinning these critics' argument that literature offers skewed 'images' of women is the confident belief that *they* know what 'real' women are like. What is not pondered is how feminist critics can detach themselves from literature, language, culture and images in order to glimpse this underlying 'truth'. Moreover, their rather joyless stance towards literature makes it difficult to understand why it is that anyone would bother to read the texts it castigates in the first place. How *do* women get seduced by literature into taking on 'limiting self-images'? A simple feminist critique of 'images of women' seems unable to tell us.

'Goblin Market' itself, on the other hand, is rather good on the subject of being charmed into ingesting something which is harmful to you. Let's return to the poem. From its very opening it sucks us in:

> Morning and evening
> Maids heard the goblins cry:
> "Come buy, come buy:
> Apples and quinces,
> Lemons and oranges,
> Plump unpecked cherries,
> Melons and raspberries,
> Bloom-down-cheeked peaches,
> Swart-headed mulberries,
> Wild free-born cranberries,
> Crab-apples, dewberries,
> Pine-apples, blackberries,
> Apricots, strawberries;-
> All ripe together
> In summer weather,- ...." (l.1–16)

As we begin to read 'Goblin Market' it's not the *images* of the maids which arrest our attention. We don't see Laura and Lizzie.

Rather, we are made into them. Like them, we are compelled to listen to the cry of the goblins calling out their wares, cramming in nouns to a list which piles up its plenty to the point of excess and threatens to overwhelm the (thirty-one-line-long) opening sentence it inhabits. But, since we are reading the poem, we are not simply listening to the cry but also uttering its 'iterated jingle' (l.233) ourselves, tugged along with a gathering momentum as the rhythm resolves itself for a moment at least into a surge of dactyls.

'Distancing ourselves' from the poem – as Cornillon suggests we should – seems almost impossible then. But our sympathies and identifications when we read it are complicated. Who are we – as readers – like? In so far as it's already written, the poem, like the goblins' cry, is something we are subject to, just as the maids 'hear' it half against their wills. On the other hand, to the extent that we must also actively engage with it and mouth its words, we are more like the goblins, seducers rather than seduced. Our relationship to the fruit is similarly hard to place. In one sense, the fruit is flaunted before us in all its plump perfection, our eyes running down that heaped-up pile of 'berries' as though over the wares on a market stall. On the other hand *enunciating* this list entails quite a lot of mouth, tongue, lip and palate work. Try it. These goblin goods demand the gift of the gab, and as we throw ourselves into the reading we relish already the pleasure it promises, chewing over rather than simply viewing the fruit. There's something about 'Goblin Market', then, that allows us to have our fruit and eat it. And that is the logic of the story itself too. Through Lizzie's heroism, Laura is able to escape the penalties usually suffered by women indulging their appetites, and is returned, despite her fall, to a state of maidenly purity. And her cure comes about through the very same means through which she's been poisoned – through tasting the fruit. Rather like the reader of the poem, then – but unlike Jeannie, who, we are told, succumbed, wasted away, and died – Laura is able to have it both ways, to enjoy the fruit and escape its consequences.

Whereas 'images of women' criticism boils literature down to 'good' and 'bad' female role models, reading the poem more closely demands that we view it as a complex entity pulling us in, but also pulling against itself, tugging in different directions simultaneously. It gives a pleasure that it also prohibits, it catches us up in what it cautions against. And who or where 'we' are as we read – maid or goblin, hungry spectator or greedy consumer – is not certain either. This less distanced reading of the poem actually calls for a subtler approach to its gender politics. We need to find a way of reading which can acknowledge that the poem endorses repressive attitudes towards women, while registering equally that its language bursts irrepressibly through such constraints. And we also need to think more about how the very experience of reading the poem inflects our own sense of gendered identity.

## Gynocriticism

To meet our first requirement we might turn here to the feminists known as 'gynocritics'. These English and American critics, writing mainly in the 1970s and 1980s, moved away from the simple, binary, positive/negative politics of 'images of women' criticism, and paid more careful literary-critical attention to literature as they found it, with all its contradictions and tensions. The 'gyno-' points to the fact that they focused their attention solely on *women's* writing, exploring the particular situations and challenges women writers negotiated in their literature. The term was coined by Elaine Showalter in an article written in 1981 and entitled 'Feminist Criticism in the Wilderness'. It describes, she writes:

> the study of women writers *as writers*, and its subjects are the history, styles, themes, genres, and structures of writing by

women; the psychodynamics of female creativity; the trajectory of the individual or collective female career; and the evolution and laws of a female literary tradition. (Showalter 1981, 184–85)

Showalter herself practised such criticism, outlining and exploring the 'female literary tradition' in her book *A Literature of their Own from Charlotte Brontë to Doris Lessing* (1977). This innovative work of scholarship reads well-known novelists such as George Eliot and Virginia Woolf alongside neglected writers such as Margaret Oliphant or G. B. Stern, restoring the latter to public notice, and tracing lines of descent, interrelationships and developments across the two-century history it outlines. Showalter's work has reinstated many neglected writers in the literary canon.

But the gynocritics who might help us best to explore women's literature in ways that don't close down its nuances are Sandra Gilbert and Susan Gubar, who, in their jointly authored book *The Madwoman in the Attic* (1979), attempt to discover the particular qualities which characterize nineteenth-century women's writing. They begin their analysis by agreeing with their feminist foremothers that stultifying images of women are woven through our (male) literary history. The first long section of their study is given over to a patient, learned and witty survey of these images in the work of an eclectic range of male writers, including Goethe, Dickens, D. G. Rossetti, Thackeray, Spenser and Swift. They suggest that – complex though the writing they gather together might be – in its treatment of women it falls into a simple, pernicious, either/or structure, in which women are cast either as 'angels' or as 'monsters'.

This is the situation in which the woman writer must take up her pen. As Gilbert and Gubar put it: '[W]hether she is a passive angel or an active monster [...] the woman writer feels herself to be literally or figuratively crippled by the debilitating alternatives her culture offers her' (Gilbert and Gubar 2000, 57). How is a female author to write? Just as, when we began to read 'Goblin Market', we were coerced by it, necessarily taking in the fruit it advertised, so women within patriarchy have no choice but to assimilate the images of women they read. If femininity is always fictionalized, what kind of literary fiction will a woman write? This is the question Gilbert and Gubar ask – and strive to answer through reading a series of nineteenth-century women writers, from Jane Austen to Emily Dickinson.

The answer they come up with is cunning in its very simplicity. They argue that women writers *employ* the divided angel/ monster imagery which is their problematic lot, but use it subversively to their own ends. Just as Lizzie co-opts the goblin fruit, transforming it from poison to cure, so women writers can wrest fictionalized accounts of femininity from male control and make them work for them. We can clarify this by looking at how Gilbert and Gubar read 'Goblin Market'. What they suggest is that the 'moral' story of transgression, suffering and redemption, and the representation of Lizzie as a demure, selfless Victorian woman, are actually only the aspects of the *surface* of the story, covering over more subversive energies, which are embodied in the riotous goblins themselves. These, they claim, are not to be read as 'sexually charismatic men' but rather as instances of 'the desirous little creatures so many women writers have recorded encountering in the haunted glens of their own minds, hurrying scurrying furry ratlike *its* or *ids*, inescapable *incubi*' (570). The goblins incarnate the repressed, monstrous, demonized aspects of femininity. Thus the poem, by appearing to warn against the goblins, is able to give full voice to them, relishing their vigour and their eccentricities, their freedom to do and say as they wish. For Gilbert and Gubar, then, the poem does still juxtapose the demure with the indecorous, and it does still ostensibly endorse feminine propriety and punish unfeminine desire. However, as a poem by a woman, it actually revels in hungry and heedless urges even while seeming to deny them.

Here we have, then, an account of the poem which remains true to its ambivalent qualities – to the tug between the pleasure it gives, and the repressive warnings against enjoyment it utters. This textual tension is, Gilbert and Gubar argue, a particular feature of the writing of women within patriarchal societies. Women's writing, they claim, sneaks past the patriarchal censors by appearing to be well behaved, and to advocate angelic femininity. But underneath it lie libidinous, revolutionary impulses, usually embodied in monstrous, grotesque or socially inappropriate figures. They sum up this general argument as follows:

> Women from Jane Austen and Mary Shelley to Emily Brontë and Emily Dickinson produced literary works that are in some sense palimpsestic, works whose surface designs conceal or obscure deeper, less accessible (and less socially acceptable) levels of meaning. Thus these authors managed the difficult task of achieving true female literary authority by simultaneously conforming to and subverting patriarchal literary standards. (73)

Women's writing, for Gilbert and Gubar, is characterized by a secretive, double quality. It is like a palimpsest: a manuscript in which a partially concealed or erased older text is overwritten, but not fully obscured, by a newer and more legible one. The feminist literary critic's job is to decipher this obscure script; to recover the covert expressions of anger from beneath the apparently demure textual veneer. Her analysis should point out and explore the elements in a text which are ostensibly held up for disapprobation – its evil, mad, monstrous or rebellious characters – and read these as embodying a subversive female potential.

Let's reflect on these arguments. This gynocritical approach offers a powerful and relatively nuanced way of reading women's writing. Unlike the rather naive 'images of women' critiques, it neither parcels literary texts out into 'good' and 'bad' models, nor demands of literature that it represent 'life' at its truest. It takes on women's writing as it is, and attempts to describe its qualities and its treatment of gendered assumptions. It certainly seems better able to account for the ambivalent qualities we read in 'Goblin Market' and the way that, as a poem, it permits the very enjoyment it prohibits.

Nevertheless, there are seductive lures in this way of reading which we might do well to resist. For a start, it seems to suggest that a double, 'palimpsestic' quality is an exclusive feature of *women*'s writing. The implication is that when a male writer employs an opposition between the 'angelic' and the 'monstrous' he is simply perpetuating sexist models, whereas when a woman does it she is necessarily using the monstrous aspects of her writing to vent her spleen and bypass the censors. We might wonder how a text like Robert Louis Stevenson's *Dr. Jekyll and Mr Hyde* (1886) – which describes two *male* characters, one virtuous and one demonic – fits into this model.

This rather blinkered, separatist approach leads to the sweeping implication that all men have one set of interests and concerns and that all women have another, and that each writes accordingly. That men might find fixed stereotypes of masculinity and femininity as troubling and as oppressive as do women is not an idea this criticism can entertain. Conversely, gynocritics find it hard to tolerate the idea that women might not all share the same sentiments or desires. Ironically, then, a criticism written in the name of female emancipation can end up being as straitjacketing as the approaches it opposes.

## Other readings

Let's return to 'Goblin Market' to explore the kinds of direction this homogenizing aspect of gynocriticism forecloses. Other readings are eminently possible. For example, we could easily suggest that Rossetti's poem, written in the midst of the

Industrial Revolution, describes the shift from an agrarian to an urban economy. It charts and condemns the move from the self-sufficiency of rural life, in which the women milk their own cows and tend their poultry, make their own bread and churn their own butter (l. 200–8) to a capitalist, 'market' driven economy, in which flashy variety and choice come at the expense of losing one's autonomy, putting oneself into the hands of unscrupulous 'merchant men'. The ostensible luxury of endless choice provided by this 'free market' is actually revealed to be a rather wearying sameness – the fruit are, unnaturally, 'all ripe together/in summer weather' (l. 16), the rhythms of the seasons no longer respected. And since, in a capitalist society, things no longer have an intrinsic worth, valuable for how they fit into the fabric of life, but instead an abstract *exchange* value, these 'goods' do not satisfy need, but simply provoke endless desire.

Thus might run a more 'socialist' account of the poem. This kind of reading, as we discussed in chapter 4, is interested in the economic underpinnings and assumptions of literary fictions. But a socialist analysis need not preclude or trump a 'gendered' reading. Indeed it might very well open one up – asking us to think about the ways in which economic and social shifts affect the relations between the sexes, and the position of women in particular. Free market economics and increasing specialization and mechanization of labour produced an increasing number of leisured middle-class women evincing much the same lassitude as does Laura after her encounters with the fruit market. We might wonder, however, whether working-class women had the same time to indulge in 'passionate yearning' and also whether their desires, and the objects of their anger and resentment, were the same as those of their more affluent 'sisters'. These are the kinds of questions which *socialist feminists* (such as Pamela Boumelha (1999), or the Marxist-Feminist Literature Collective (1978)) might ask of 'Goblin Market'.

Our further readings of 'Goblin Market' here can allow us to gather together, and reflect further upon, our reservations about the gynocritical approach to literature. They all come down once again to questions of *difference*. Gynocriticism, despite its liberating agenda, seems to make assumptions which operate coercively, forcing all women – and all literature – into a single mould. This is always the risk of ways of reading literature which work from the basis of some presumed 'identity'. Here, a feminist 'identity politics' implicitly assumes that women are all fundamentally alike – rather as Rossetti describes the apparently identical Lizzie and Laura: 'Like two flakes of new-fall'n snow' (l. 188). Rossetti's poem shows, however, that their ostensible 'likeness' conceals considerable differences in experience, desire and character. If Lizzie and Laura, our alliteratively-linked and almost indistinguishable sisterly allies, are different from one another, it would seem misguided to assume that Rossetti's fundamental feelings and meanings are the same as those of Charlotte Brontë, George Eliot, Elizabeth Barrett Browning or Emily Dickinson; to assume that all women writers feel, and write, in fundamentally the same ways. The gynocritics are, in their politics, *liberal* – inheritors of the tradition that, asserting the untrammelled freedoms of the individual, goes back to the economic theories of John Stuart Mill. As later feminists have pointed out, 'liberal feminism' is largely a middle-class, white, Western movement, even while it assumes in a lofty and imperialist manner that the qualities and concerns of the 'individual' whose rights it protests are universal.

If we can criticize gynocriticism for its political naiveties in lumping all women together, we can also suggest that its approach to literature is stolidly unifying. Gilbert and Gubar acknowledge, of course, that texts are duplicitous – their very theory is grounded on that possibility. But the model of the *palimpsest* they use implies that we can bypass one level of signification to discern the 'true' meaning beneath – which invariably, in their readings of writers as diverse as Jane Austen and Emily Dickinson, turns out to be the cry of 'passionate yearning' and 'balked desire' (l. 266–7) under the demure exterior. The textual surface covers over – in each case – the same hidden 'depth'. Their approach to gender is explicitly 'anti-essentialist'. They criticize the way in which women are forced into a single patriarchal mould and 'constructed' by patriarchal ideology. But they seem to tear down one fixed picture of womanhood, only to posit a profounder essence in its place. This need not necessarily be a problem – but a more sustained reading of 'Goblin Market' might certainly throw it into question.

The gynocritics' quest for a covert, true, female meaning has at least three unfortunate and interrelated effects for a reading of Rossetti's poem. First, by paring it down to a single sense, it ignores the possibilities for alternative readings the poem continually solicits. Second, this reduction also treats all other aspects of the poem as inessential fripperies – whereas some of the most striking features of 'Goblin Market' are its repetitions, half-rhymes, alliteration and awkward rhythms, along with the way it describes things through piled up and proliferating similes. Third, by thus ignoring the texture and movement of the poem, a gynocritical approach seems to bypass too any question of the sensuous, dynamic, tactile and temporal experience of reading it. The poem is viewed as a product not a process, and the reader therefore simply a consumer on the meaning-market rather than someone who works with, while being caught up and altered by, its rhythms and exigencies. We've already seen how, as we began to read the opening of 'Goblin Market', it was no longer clear who 'we' were – maids, or goblins, seducers or seduced. The very experience of reading started to work over the fixed oppositions of gender difference. We might argue then that gynocriticism, by appealing to the specificity of *female* experience, seems to ignore the yet more singular experience of reading, an experience in which 'my' identity is no longer certain and alters as I read.

In short, then, a gynocritical approach seems to be faithful neither to the differences between women, nor the differences within literature. And these twin blindnesses are bound up with one another. Both work on the assumption that we can simply move beneath the frivolous superficialities of appearance or style to reveal the real woman and the true meaning. In fact for these critics the real woman *is* the true meaning. What our reflections on this approach seem to suggest, though, is that we need to find a less unifying, more fluid, way of understanding both gender and literature, if we are not to end up perpetuating precisely the kind of tyrannical thinking we sought to oppose.

## Difference feminists

It was feminist intellectuals thinking and writing in France from the late 1970s onwards who first argued that a belief in fixed meanings and identities – even if held in the name of women's rights – reinforced patriarchal ideologies. The writers Hélène Cixous and Luce Irigaray are often referred to as the 'French feminists', though neither is native to France, and both have questioned the value of the feminist label. What links them more than the French language is how each aims to think in more varied ways about the sexed self and its relationship to signification. They suggest that there is a tight link between a way of reading which searches for a fundamental meaning, and patriarchal ways of thinking about sexual difference. And the term they use to describe this link is *phallogocentrism*. This coinage is a hybrid of 'logocentrism' – the belief that meaning is grounded in a single word or words (logos) rather than emerging through a weave of significations – and phallocentrism – a way of thinking which, as we will discuss more in a moment, privileges the phallus as the guarantor of sexual identity. I'm going to read and discuss their ideas in some detail here, before returning to 'Goblin Market'.

The 'difference feminists' explore a range of thinkers of sexual difference, but a point of connection is Freud. Cixous writes in an essay called 'Sorties' (1975) that Freud:

> starts from what he calls the *anatomical* difference between the sexes. And we know how that is pictured in his eyes: as the difference between having/not having the phallus. (2000, 268)

Freud is certainly not unique in thinking about anatomical difference in this way. And it might well seem to us that he gives an obvious and undeniable account of it. It is incontestable that a man has a penis and that a woman doesn't. But what Cixous asks is why the penis has to be what we start with. Freud's hierarchical, either/or model of sexual difference is based on the assumption that the possession of the penis is the neutral 'first' state, from which differences can be gauged. As we suggested in chapter 5, his account of identity as being formed through the 'Oedipus complex' and through 'castration anxiety' seems to work far better for boys than it does for girls. What Cixous points out is that Freud's 'neutral' 'scientific' conclusions are skewed from the outset by the methods employed. Sexual difference is established through *looking*, through *sight*. Since males have visible sexual organs, this mode of perception implicitly imagines women as lacking something. Here we see already the slippage from biological sex to a culturally determined characterisation of gender, which nevertheless takes itself as natural. But the privilege Freud accords to sight can be questioned.

We can turn to Irigaray at this juncture. She takes on the phallocentrism of Freud's account through proposing an alternative story about the genesis of gender difference. She wonders what would happen if we tried to imagine anatomical difference experienced through other senses – if we privileged touch, rather than sight, for example. Suddenly, things change:

> In order to touch himself, man needs an instrument: his hand, a woman's body, language … And this self-caressing requires at least a minimum of activity. As for woman, she touches herself in and of herself without any need for mediation, and before there is any way to distinguish activity from passivity. Woman "touches herself" all the time, and moreover no one can forbid her to do so, for her genitals are formed of two lips in continuous contact. Thus, within herself, she is already two – but not divisible into one(s) – that caress each other. (1985, 24)

This passage is explicit, risqué and perhaps risible. But it is also a rather brilliant riposte to Freud. Woman is no longer envisioned as lacking something: her genitals are multiple and involved, rather than either present and singular or simply lacking. Now it is man who is seen as in need of something extra, while woman, languorously, has all she wants. Irigaray's *tactile* 'reading' of sexed bodies turns the tables. Starting from the woman's experience, it defines the man in relation to that. *He* is now secondary, subsequent and deficient. Irigaray doesn't necessarily suggest that this account is any truer – but it is at least as persuasive. It is possible to think about things from the other side.

In fact, if we think further about the implications of what Irigaray writes, we can see that she does more than simply reversing the direction of either/or identity thinking. In tipping the approach to sexual difference on its head she transforms everything, including – and especially – the way we think about difference itself. For if we accept that the female experiences her body as already containing difference within itself, then *this* model of sexual difference does not need to juxtapose itself to a secondary other. We no longer require an either/or, angel/monster, masculine/feminine, active/passive way of thinking about the world. Irigaray imagines more various and more primordial kinds of difference – differences as (self-)relationships that are there from the start, likenesses that aren't quite identities. Beginning by re-imagining the female body, replacing fearful misogynist versions of the female genitals as a lack and absence with a reading of them as plural and touching, she points the way towards thinking about sexual difference itself in ways that aren't simply oppositional. The possibilities she points to might, in that case, be as liberating for men as for women, allowing for a range of differences to be tolerated rather than forcing everything into the same mould. We might further point out that none of these arguments is simply made *against* Freud. Rather, both Cixous and Irigaray read Freud through Freud, exploring what is repressed or pushed to one side in his own accounts of sexual difference, in order to liberate the possibilities of psychoanalysis in new terms.

Cixous concurs with Irigaray's argument that refiguring sexual difference will be freeing for men as well as women:

> Phallocentrism is the enemy. Of *everyone*. Men stand to lose by it, differently but as seriously as women. [...] And it is time to transform. (268)

That call for *transformation* is echoed by Irigaray, and here both women's thinking joins up with more explicitly literary concerns. They suggest that one of the best places to go to find rigid categories troubled, and fixed oppositions blurred, is literature. And they dream of – and practise themselves – kinds of writing, and ways of reading, which cultivate likenesses that aren't identities, celebrate differences that aren't oppositions, and appeal to senses other than that of sight. Cixous describes this transformative writing as *écriture féminine* (a female or feminine writing) and Irigaray – talking of something similar – appeals to a *parler-femme*, a womanspeak.

For neither of these feminists, however, are these modes of writing the exclusive property of women. The very fact of starting out from (apparently 'feminine') plurality and fluidity will wash away too fixed a demarcation between 'the masculine' and the 'feminine'. Cixous argues, indeed, that there is no genuine writing without a 'bisexual' mixture, without plural identities and significations. And writing itself permits and demands such mixing of meanings and identities:

> Writing is the passageway, the entrance, the exit, the dwelling place of the other in me – the other that I am and am not, that I don't know how to be, but that I feel passing, that makes me live – that tears me apart, disturbs me, changes me, who? a feminine one, a masculine one, some? (Sorties, 269)

Cixous's own writing enacts what she describes here, blurring the boundary line between theory and practice, between her writing and the writing she is writing *about*. And what she is writing about is precisely a writing which itself smudges boundaries while making connections.

We have already described the opening of 'Goblin Market' in ways which jibe with the fecund ideas of the difference feminists. We talked about how getting our tongues around the list of fruits which first meets the eye makes reading it an experience which fuses sight and taste. And we also suggested that as we read we are at times made into maidens and at others bewitched into goblins, our identifications neither fully with one nor the other. We can now suggest that these features of its writing have a transformative potential, foregrounding the ways in which gender can be altered, inflected, worked over and modified.

When we read someone's writing our own 'I' merges with and inhabits other selves, ceaselessly rehearsing alternative possibilities. Before we think very much about *what* we read, then, there is something about the very experience and process of reading which is on the side of the fluidity and plurality Irigaray and Cixous celebrate. But Rossetti's poem also exemplifies these qualities in its own more particular and idiomatic ways. Generically, the poem is a strange hybrid, not fitting clearly into a type. Its nursery-rhyme or fairy-tale elements blend with a *Genesis*-story about forbidden fruit. In turn, this story of the Fall melds into a more contemporary fall narrative, invoking the 'fallen woman' plot that was the stuff of Victorian melodrama and domestic romance, as it recalls Jeannie, Laura's precursor in transgression 'who should have been a bride;/But who for joys brides hope to have/Fell sick and died' (l.313–5). The Fall and the fall both then get taken up and redeemed in a feminized-Gospel story, the flawless Lizzie saving her lost sister: her language, as she offers up her juice-smeared body, echoes Christ's at the Last Supper 'Eat me, drink me, love me;/Laura make much of me' (l.471–2). But this communion scene is too juicy to be purely spiritual: its language is eroticized, merging fluidly into an image of *sexual* communion. 'Hug me, kiss me, suck my juices' (l.468) Lizzie urges Laura, who 'kissed and kissed her with a hungry mouth' (l.492). Here along with all the other generic and moral distinctions the poem has transgressed, it overrides too the incest taboo, that prohibition on relationship between people too alike.

As we follow these meanderings, mergings and mutations we might recall, as many feminists have done, that the word 'genre' comes from the same root as the word for gender. Indeed in French the same signifier does for both. Genre, like gender, divides things into different types and kinds, but both are also *generative* (another word generated from the same source). 'Goblin Market' is the fruit of a series of literary couplings and liaisons. It takes its place in a literary genealogy, but is no dutiful daughter; its genre is *sui generis*, its own, a new possibility, a transformation.

The proliferation of differences we see incarnated in the poem's genres can also be *heard* in its rhymes. Rhymes always work by making a connection between otherwise unlike things – they bridge a difference by making a relationship. 'Goblin Market' reverberates with rhymes, but it never settles into a regular pattern: any attempt to mark it aabb, abab, or according to any other measure, will founder. And the poem cultivates different *kinds* of rhymes. Often we can link these to aspects of the poem's meanings. The goblins' fruit cry employs what John Lennard has called 'auto-rhyme' (1996, 92) in its simple repetition of the same word "berries/-berries/-berries/-berries/-berries' (l.10–14). As we've said, the apparent variety the goblins promise can also be read as a wearying sameness; and this we can now see borne out in these stuck-sounding repetitions. The opening of the poem also employs *rime riche* – a rhyme on words that have identical sounds but different senses, as in 'pass by// come buy' (17/19). Through sharing the same sound, 'pass by' haunts the injunction to buy, suggesting the transitoriness of the pleasure that would be purchased, just as the word 'fruit' promises enjoyment, but also consequences. The accord of full rhymes has similar effects, 'flowers' in line 150, for example, haunted by 'hours' (152) so that their withering is already hinted at. The lesser resemblances of half or imperfect rhymes ' upbraidings/maidens' can jar, upbraiding us by clashing dissonantly with the innocent appearance of things.

Sound echoes sense then, but vice versa too. Sounds generate significations unthought of before and there is a continual cross-pollination between the two. And that simple fact is perhaps more remarkable than any single sense we can gather from Rossetti's rhymes. The poem demonstrates through its haunted and haunting echo-chamber of rhymes that strange graftings can bear fruit, and that relationships do not have to follow strict patterns or rules in order to generate meanings and possibilities. Rhymes cultivate accidental, inessential features of language – producing couples from chance resemblances, rather than enforcing sameness on the basis of a pre-given identity.

Liaisons happen at the even less meaningful level of the letter too. The poem revels in alliteration, and its two main characters, of course, are alliteratively linked. The capital 'L' which begins both their proper names, as it also commences so many of the poem's lines, is like two capital 'I's, one erect, one fallen, touching while diverging from one another, neither single nor double. And uttering it makes us feel this too, puts us in relation with ourselves as we touch our tongues to the roof of our mouths. The letter 'L' is – to borrow some more goblin words –'sweet to tongue' (l.30). Indeed that phrase itself thrills with internal differences and senses both active and passive: it is not clear whether the fruit is, in a passive sense, sweet to the tongue or whether, tipping tongue into an active verb, it is sweet to tongue the fruit. And if tongue is a verb, then it can refer equally to tasting, touching and talking.

In its mixing of genres and in the minutiae of its rhymes, in its alliterations and its reversible phrasings, then, 'Goblin Market' seems to give us the heterogeneous and labile writing Cixous and Irigaray call for. Rossetti plays across a whole spectrum of differences that aren't oppositions, and shows that like forms can be very different, and unlike things can nevertheless exist in productive relationship. The approach to reading of the 'difference feminists' seems to be able to register and celebrate this play in ways that the other feminist theories we've explored fail to achieve. Reading 'Goblin Market' with an eye not only on its 'images' but on the shape of its letters and the patterns they trace, as well as an ear for its sonorities, emphases and dissonances, and a feel for its texture and how it tangs on the tongue, seems to respect more fully its 'literary' qualities than do the other critical approaches we have explored, while also bringing our own bodies – the felt experience of reading – into play. Getting close to the poem, we also touch ourselves – and never one without the other.

Pleasure and politics are no longer mutually exclusive here. A feminist argument for the importance of senses other than that of sight allows for a more exquisite registering of the pleasure of reading, while also working over our understanding of identity.

The differences we have just discussed seem no longer distinguishable into a gendered binary between masculine and feminine identities, nor into other didactic polarities of good and bad, or angelic and demonic. The poem's generic mutations intermingle the spiritual and the corporeal, ancient stories with the modern ones, childish lore with adult erotica, and its rhymes and alliterations create all manner of eccentric alliances and hybrids. But this very fact might give us pause. There is a risk that too rhapsodic a revelling in plurality and heterogeneity will take us so close to the poem that we lose sight of the inescapable fact that at a narrative level it does seem broadly to endorse renunciation and repression and does broadly support feminine virtue. The poem ends, after all, with Laura recounting her long ago goblin adventures to her own children, as an instructive moral tale. We have been suggesting in local ways that difference and sameness must be related, but have not yet brought this insight to bear on our reading of the poem as a larger whole. Indeed, we might even suggest that our discussion of difference is itself rather undifferentiated. By celebrating its potentially subversive properties we have failed to think about how something can only be subversive within a context which makes it so. 'Goblin Market' does open up vistas of possibilities – but within the frame of an ostensibly didactic story. Simply to be mesmerized by its abundance is perhaps to be too Laura-like, too bewitched by choice for its own sake and sucked therefore into a strung-out state where it is impossible to gather anything together.

One criticism often made of the 'difference feminists', is that the writing they celebrate and practise comes too close to the kinds of (feminized) speech that has no purchase in the world – hysteria, mad ravings, babble. That both Cixous and Irigaray continue to write and to have profound effects on thinking about the liaisons between sexual differences and literature, would seem to refute that argument. Their writing makes clear and cogent claims, at the same time as opening out the tactile, connotative aspects of writing – the way it hooks up with itself, resonates and proliferates untameably. But it might nevertheless be helpful to look at some other accounts of gender, sexual difference and literature that take up in other styles and contexts the question of the relationship between a feminist literary practice and the cultural frame within which it occurs.

# Feminism & deconstruction

Feminists such as Julia Kristeva, Judith Butler, Eve Sedgwick and Diane Elam, each in different ways, pay attention to the ways in which difference, movement, play and potential must be related to the dominant, apparently rigid and unified, context from which it emerges. The name 'deconstruction' was coined by Derrida, whose writings each of these women engages with, to condense this idea, pointing *at once* to constructions *and* to how they de-generate.

Judith Butler, in her book *Gender Trouble*, thinks about gender precisely in terms of a simultaneous movement of construction and degeneration. We inherit particular identity models, particular constructions of masculinity and femininity, from our culture. This is inevitable. We cannot operate or make meanings except through the language, structures and ideas into which we are born. We can't, then, simply lift ourselves outside constructions of gendered identity. But – Butler suggests – gender is not thoroughly straitjacketing. It is not like a dress – or muzzle – that we put on once and for all. Since we exist and make our meanings in time, so gender is a set of behaviours which have to be '*iterated*' (l.233) (to borrow another word from 'Goblin Market') through time. I can't simply be feminine *once*. I need to keep doing it. And to repeat something – as we saw in Rossetti's use of auto-rhyme – can *either* consolidate it, *or* undermine it and thus alter it. If gendered identities need to be repeated, then they can always be repeated slightly differently. Butler refers to 'the performative possibilities for proliferating gender configurations outside the restricting frames of masculinist domination' (1990, 141). This sentence, full of polysyllabic plosives, is rather pompous and off-putting. Her *examples* bring out better the parodic possibilities she's thinking of. She talks about drag artists – men who dress up as women. Ordinarily, we would think about them as *mimicking* femininity. Butler suggests, however, that the drag artist exposes the fact that femininity is always a performance – always a series of acts. For Butler, this exposé of the artifice of femininity doesn't return us to some more natural, pre-theatrical state. There is no 'true' female identity, prior to the language and culture in which we speak and act. But it does, Butler suggests, allow us to think about how femininity might be performed and repeated *otherwise* – how we might change and modify the script that culture gives us.

Again, let us relate this to 'Goblin Market'. One of the moments when it seems most clearly to describe ideal feminine behaviour is when it talks about Laura and Lizzie tending to their domestic duties. The poet describes how they

> Fetched in honey, milked the cows,
> Aired and set to rights the house,
> Kneaded cakes of whitest wheat,
> Cakes for dainty mouths to eat,
> Next churned butter, whipped up cream,
> Fed their poultry, sat and sewed;
> Talked as modest maidens should:
> Lizzie with an open heart,
> Laura in an absent dream,
> One content, one sick in part. (l.203–212).

Both go through the motions of maidenly duty. They *both* talk and act 'as modest maidens should'. But what this passage therefore reveals is that such maidenly behaviour can be performed whether you are consciously there behind it (as Lizzie is) or simply, like Laura, going through the motions. In this sense, the behaviour emerges as a set of 'acts' detached from any underlying identity. Similarly that rather pious phrase 'talked as modest maidens should' undercuts itself. The conditional 'should' has the force of a prescription, but it also admits doubt, and the possibility that maidens *might* act otherwise. We can extrapolate from this local linguistic point to make a larger 'deconstructive' argument about power: the moment power needs to enforce itself, through laws, rules and prescriptions, it also renders itself visible and open to challenge. To have to articulate how maidens should talk is to suggest that they don't naturally or essentially do so, and thus to cause us to ask *why* they 'should'. To have to assert the nature of someone's identity – to repeat what they are really like, or what they ought to be like, is to suggest some anxiety as to whether that identity is really there.

Deconstructive feminist criticism such as Butler's attempts to keep an eye and an ear out for what, within the very establishment of an identity or the attribution of an essence, renders it provisional, and open to transformation and alteration. In 'Goblin Market' we gain our sense of the identities of both maidens and goblins through the way in which they are repeatedly likened to other things. Simile is this poem's most frequently employed trope. It expands the 567 lines of 'Goblin Market' so that it contains a whole bestiary of creatures and bouquets of flowers – cats, rats, ratels and wombats, swans and pigeons, lilies and orange trees – not to mention the citadels and kingdoms, the deserts and armies, the waterspouts and oceans which are also conjured. It seems to be part of the playful permutation of possibilities the poem is hospitable to. But it opens these out on the basis of a continual intoning of the word 'like' – a word that is in fact repeated so often that it becomes rather uncanny. At the moment when Rossetti describes the apparently identical Lizzie and Laura, its eeriness becomes almost oppressive. They are 'Like two blossoms on one stem,/Like two flakes of new-fall'n snow/Like two wands of ivory' (l.189–90). The word 'like' starts to warp here. The sisters are described as being like things which are themselves alike – two snowflakes, two blossoms and so on. An endless reduplication of likeness is how 'gender identity' is perpetuated – women behave like their mothers and sisters, and like the images of women represented to them. Gender is instituted, Butler says, through a *'stylized repetition of acts'* (140). But in fact there is something necessarily approximate about 'likeness', and it is telling that Rossetti insists on this likeness after Laura's 'fall' and hence at the moment when it is starting to come apart. A likeness is precisely *not* an identity, but a resemblance. Difference is fundamental to it, as it is to identity formation – but the possibility of flaws, gaps and unravellings within ostensible identities is, consequently, there from the start.

The possibility for difference within likeness is – the poem suggests – always there. And this of course is a 'feminist' possibility – the possibility that things might be otherwise, that the likeness between members of a sex is not an identity, but a provisional relationship which also allows for differences, just as sexual differences can permit and solicit other alliances and organizations. This possibility, though, is only there if we mark it. And that, perhaps, is the final thing about 'Goblin Market' that we should remark. It is a poem fascinated and worked by repetition, and it is also the kind of poem that demands to be read again and again. It appeals to a childish pleasure in repetition – and it also ends with a moment that *represents* that. The poem ends with Laura telling her daughters and nieces the story we have just read ourselves, a story of 'those pleasant days long gone/Of not returning time' (l.549–50). This ending has often been read as offering a rather saccharine conclusion to a subversive and stirring tale. 'There is no friend like a sister' (l. 562) Laura concludes, as though sisterhood is where all similes, and the possibilities for difference they offer, fail. But its emphasis on retelling an account of sisterhood for new generations is one that feminists have long emphasized, and continue to today, in a world in which, as Diane Elam says, there is 'talk that feminism is yesterday's news' (2000, 83). Elam goes on to argue that 'feminism continues to be effective ... because its repetition also produces revisions' (84) and that 'it is repeated over time, yet never quite the same' (100). 'Goblin Market', in its cultivation of repetitions and differences at all levels, tells us that too. By ending with a scene in which its story is repeated in a new context, it opens itself to the future, and to the new readings which it will continue to engender.

# 7

# Literature and empire

In this chapter we will focus on literature's relationship to matters at once global and local – to empire and colonialism, to race and ethnicity, and to the earth. And we'll do this through reading H. Rider Haggard's *She* (1887) – a late-nineteenth-century tale of three Englishmen's adventures and misadventures in central Africa – alongside the writings of post-colonial theorists such as Edward Said, Anne McClintock, Ngugi wa Thiong'o and Homi Bhabha. These thinkers' work emerges after and reflects on the period of decolonization and independence movements in Africa, Asia and the Caribbean which followed the Second World War. Their interests are diverse – and indeed an attention *to* diversity is amongst them – but in a general way we can say that they at once seek to do justice to the voices, histories and stories which are silenced when one race, nation or part of the world dominates another; and that they analyse and criticize ways of thinking and writing which underpin and seem to justify such domination in the first place. This second aspect of their work means that, while they write *after* overt Western colonialism has ceased, they pay attention also to the imperialist histories and writings which precede it, and which continue to influence our 'postcolonial' present. Edward Said, a Palestinian-American literary critic and a theorist of colonialism and imperialism, usefully distinguishes between imperialism and colonialism thus:

> "imperialism" means the practice, the theory, and the attitudes
> of a dominating metropolitan centre ruling a distant territory;

"colonialism", which is almost always a consequence of imperialism, is the implanting of settlements on distant territory.
(1993, 8)

Imperialism, then, precedes colonialism. And many have argued
that – in different guises – it might be said to outlast it too.
Anne McClintock – taking issue with the sweeping, 'prema-
turely celebratory' term 'post-colonial' argues that 'the power
of US finance capital and huge multi-nationals to direct the
flows of capital, commodities, armaments and media information around the world can have an impact as massive as any
colonial regime' and she describes these new manifestations
of power as new 'forms of imperialism' (1992, 87). Imperialism,
then – and hence the question of literature's relationship to
it – is as worthy now of thoughtful critical attention as ever
it was.

Haggard's *She* was published in 1886–7, near the onset of the
'scramble for Africa', the moment when industrialized European
nations, who had long dominated Africa and Asia through
economic means, rushed towards a more overt acquisition and
colonization of lands and peoples. Haggard himself had taken a
hand in the process. In 1875, at the age of nineteen, he became
secretary to Sir Henry Bulwer, the lieutenant governor of Natal,
South Africa. He was involved in the British annexation of the
Transvaal, and was the person to raise the Union Jack over the
region for the first time. *She* itself is not a story about either
'imperialism' or 'colonialism' in the most literal senses. But this
strange, powerful, fantastical, sometimes funny and occasionally
ridiculous novel, which recounts the adventures of a group of
Westerners, confident in their education and supremacy,
heading to Africa in order to penetrate and plunder its mysteries, has much to tell us about empire and its fundamental
relations to literature and to writing.

## *She* and English literature

*She* – the sixth novel by Rider Haggard – is emphatically a work of English literature. Its title is a simple English pronoun, and its events are recounted in an idiomatic English by the narrator, a Cambridge don, Ludwig Horace Holly. But to open the book is to encounter a whole welter of unfamiliar scripts, strange alphabets and foreign tongues. Printed as the book's frontispiece from the first edition onwards is a 'facsimile' of a supposedly ancient potsherd (a fragment of an earthenware pot, in fact mocked up for Haggard by his sister-in-law Agnes Barber). It is covered in smudges, stains and patched-together breaks, and criss-crossed with signatures, dates and a number of polyglot scrawls, some of them in old and modern English, others in Latin of various kinds, as well as a long account in a script which – we later learn – is Uncial (old) Greek and a couple of Egyptian hieroglyphs. Each of these writings will later be faithfully repro-duced in the body of the text, too, as well as being translated for us. The opening pages of *She,* then, positively bristle with foreign languages, names, alphabets and characters. This work of English literature is interwoven from the outset with other languages.

The novel's multi-lingual beginning is multiply suggestive. For a start, the variety of scripts and languages has the effect of foregrounding the fact that the rest of the narration is in English. We would not expect the Norfolk-born Haggard to write in any other tongue, of course – his book was intended for an English readership, and his own language skills were weak. The opening of his novel, however, serves to remind us that English is but one language amongst others. That Haggard has no choice but to write mainly in English does not make his use of that language any less significant. *Which* language a story, poem or play is written in will always depend on a whole series of geo-political, historical and personal factors. It will depend on

where its author is born, or brought up, of course – and therefore on which languages are taught and spoken in that place.
And that in turn will depend upon the history of that country –
who lives there, who has invaded it or emigrated to it, which
countries trade with it, and so on.

For writers and critics from the former colonies these facts
take on a particular edge and urgency. In his book *Decolonising
the Mind: The Politics of Language in African Literature*, which he
describes as his 'farewell to English as a vehicle' for his writings
(1986, xiv), the novelist and theorist of post-colonial literature
Ngugi wa Thiong'o writes that to continue to write in the
English of his country's ex-colonizer is to continue to perpetuate colonial values. 'From now on', he vows, 'it is Gikuyu and
Kiswahili all the way'. English, he argues compellingly, through
descriptions of his own alienating education under British rule,
was imposed upon his nation, along with the literature and
cultural assumptions that go with it. 'Orature (oral literature) in
Kenyan languages stopped' (12) and was replaced by 'the works
of such geniuses of racism as a Rider Haggard or a Nicholas
Monsarrat' (19). We'll return later to the specific question of
Haggard's racism. For now the point to underscore is that the
imposition of English as the language of education in British
colonies went alongside the teaching of English – instead of
indigenous – literature, and that literature itself in this case
became a tool of domination, capable of imposing English
cultural values and ways of thinking about and seeing the world.

Other writers, while they acknowledge that language and
literature are not innocent of power, or separable from questions
of cultural and racial difference, disagree with the argument that
the language of the former colonizer should simply be repudi-
ated. They suggest that this language can always be taken up and
taken over, and modified to new ends. As the Nigerian writer
Gabriel Okara asks 'Why shouldn't there be a Nigerian or West
African English which we can use to express our own ideas,

thinking and philosophy in our own way?' (1963, 15–16).
Okara's own poetry and prose certainly attempts this. And in a
different 'post-colonial' context we might see the novels of
writers such as Salman Rushdie (1981) and Arundhati Roy
(1997) similarly offering an English inflected by the rhythms and
idioms of Indian thought and writing.

At issue in the arguments of Ngugi wa Thiong'o and Gabriel
Okara is the relationship between language, identity and domination. Both see the nature of a particular language as being linked
to cultural identity, but whereas Ngugi sees that link as being
immutable, Okara suggests a greater flexibility in which – while
a language may have been coercively imposed – once learned it
can be adapted to new ends. Haggard's much-graffitied potsherd
similarly conveys the ways in which language might dominate
but also serve its speaker or writer. The original story in the
Uncial Greek is one of passion, murder, exile and vengeance. But
the languages in which the story is translated down the ages
convey their own story and history. It's first penned by an
Egyptian woman, Amenartas, in the language of her Greek
husband, Kallikrates, and addressed to their son Tisithenes. The
'original' story, then, is already told in a tongue foreign to the
teller – one she has adopted freely, we assume, since she does so
for love. As the story and comments on it move from Greek to
Latin to French and then to medieval and modern English, we
can trace the passage of the descendants of Tisisthenes as they
move across the globe, migrating from Greece to Rome, then
settling in Lombardy, before moving with the invader
Charlemagne to Brittany, and travelling finally to Britain during
the reign of Edward the Confessor (*not* – it is interesting to note
– with William the Conquerer). In themselves, then, these
languages tell a story of exile, travel, conquest and settlement. As
Laura Chrisman has pointed out (1990), they cover the languages
of the major sources of Western 'civilization' – Egyptian, Greek,
Roman, French and English. But they also, therefore, demon-

strate how languages feed into one another – like the mutating name of the family, which alters from the Greek, to the Latin Vindex, before being anglicized as Vincey – always changing and being altered by circumstance, while outlasting and triumphing over the moment in which they were written. Language, it seems, has a dual relationship to imperial, colonial or other forms of power. On the one hand it can be violently imposed upon a subjugated people, displacing their own native tongue and the culture and ideas expressed through it. On the other hand, it can always be co-opted and altered to serve new ends, and it also has the power to outlast the human power which sought to impose it in the first place, potentially betraying that power through its own continuing testimony. In this way, stories which seem to celebrate empire can be read after the period of imperialism has passed, and read in ways which make legible the violences of the imperialism they celebrate.

What, then, of this potsherd story? It is handed down through the ages until it reaches our novel's heroes, the narrator and Cambridge don, Ludwig Horace Holly, and his young, beautiful charge, Leo Vincey, whose inheritance it is. In their study in Cambridge, upon Leo's coming of age, the two men read the tale first recounted by Amenartas. They learn how she and her husband Kallikrates fled Egypt, travelling south until they were shipwrecked off the African coast, and escorted to the beautiful white Queen of the local, Arabic-speaking, 'wild men' (36) and how the Queen fell in love with Kallikrates, attempt-ing to seduce him away from his wife by showing him a mighty flame, the 'rolling Pillar of Life' (36). Kallikrates resisted the Queen's charms and her promise of immortality and she slew him. Amenartas fled her wrath, ending up in Athens, which is where she penned her tale, addressing it to her son Tisisthenes and urging him to seek vengeance on his father's killer. This murderous and apparently immortal Queen, we will later find out, is the 'She-who-must-be-obeyed' who is referred to in the title of Haggard's novel. Documents accompanying the potsherd suggest that Leo is the last descendant of Amenartas and Kallikrates – and so he decides to take up the ancient quest, and discover for himself the Arabic-speaking tribe, their beautiful Queen and the Pillar of Life. With his learned guardian Holly and their faithful manservant Job, he therefore sets off for central Africa. The discoveries and adventures of this journey will form the main matter of the novel.

The story on the sherd is what motivates all the subsequent events of the novel. And the very act and fact of reading this story is thus crucial here. Leo and Holly are uniquely fitted to read, understand and act on the potsherd's narrative. Holly, charged with Vincey's education by the young boy's dying father, has been instructed to rear him in a knowledge of the Classics, as well – unusually – of Arabic. When Vincey comes into his inheritance at the age of twenty-five, and discovers that he is the descendant of Amenartas and Kallikrates, he is, then, at once in a position to understand the documents entrusted to him, and to undertake his quest to Africa in search of the immortal Queen and the source of eternal life. *She*, emphasizes not only the importance of language but also of *scholarship*. Haggard begins his tale in Cambridge University, and with the education and training of a young man. These facts remind us that imperialism was never simply a mercantile or military affair, but was also a matter of knowledge, research and writing. And this is a point made compellingly by Edward Said, in his important book *Orientalism* (1978) – the work often cited as the point of origin for 'post-colonial theory'.

# Edward Said and Orientalism

Edward Said focuses on a network of academic disciplines – linguistic, anthropological, historical, literary and so on – which go under the general heading of 'orientalism'. 'Orientalism' was, from the late-eighteenth century onwards, the area of study which treated the so-called 'Orient', and the information and knowledge it produced was essential to the operations of British imperialism and colonialism in Asia. This already suggests that, as a field of study, it is far from being neutral terrain, but is readily deployable by imperialist interests. To trade with let alone to rule a country, knowledge of its language, geography and customs is necessary or at least advantageous, and the desire to trade, occupy or govern a country is a powerful motive force in the acquisition of knowledge about it. But Said suggests that the relationship between such knowledge and power is even more intimate than this. Orientalism, he argues, is

> an elaboration not only of a basic geographical distinction (the world is made up of two unequal halves, Orient and Occident) but also of a whole series of "interests" which, by such means as scholarly discovery, philological reconstruction, psychological analysis, landscape and sociological description, it not only creates but also maintains; it *is*, rather than expresses, a certain *will* or *intention* to understand, in some cases to control, manipulate, even to incorporate, what is a manifestly different (or alternative and novel) world. (1995, 12)

Here Said suggests – following on from the work of Michel Foucault, who argued that power and knowledge were always intertwined (Foucault 1980) – that even before any specific knowledge of the Orient might be of use to an imperialist ruler or colonial government, the very fact of setting out to *know* the Orient is already an act of power. In fact it is to be involved in a coercive fabrication, through assuming that there is an entity called the Orient to be known. By carving up the world into two halves, one of which claims to know the other, orientalism itself forever fixes that 'other half' *as* an object of knowledge.

Every description of 'the Orient' serves to enforce the idea that it *has* a fixed, identifiable and intrinsic set of properties. What is effaced is the fact that the 'geographical distinction' of the world into 'two unequal halves' is in the first instance an arbitrary act. Said writes that 'the Orient is not an inert fact of nature ... [but] an idea that has a history and a tradition of thought, imagery and vocabulary that have given it reality and presence in and for the West' (4–5). 'The East' is not simply a place, but a position, described always in relation to what is west of it. Knowledge of 'the East' must always entail a knower, who inhabits his/her own geographical location, and whose 'knowledge' of other cultures therefore emerges from an implicit set of assumptions determined by his/her own culture. Said suggests that these assumptions – for example about what language, reality, psychology and so on *are* – are implicitly taken as a norm against which the East is measured and objectified.

Further consequences ensue from this. Said shows how, on the basis of their own assumptions of a norm, Western orientialists lump together a whole range of supposedly deviant qualities and properties, which are assumed, in extremely generalized and stereotypical terms, to belong to the Oriental. Thus the idea of the Orient 'accrues a wide field of meaning, associations and connotations' (203) – ideas of 'Oriental despotism, Oriental sensuality' and so on – which emerge through the attempt to define a huge terrain of land, and a diversity of cultures, from within the assumptions and limitations of the orientalist's own point of departure.

When we read Western literature then, it can be illuminating to consider its relationship to 'the East' – the ways in which it claims to know the East, the symbolic uses to which 'the Orient' or 'oriental' characters are put, or, conversely, the ways in which the West's economic dependence on trade, including the slave trade, colonization and imperialism are glossed over, suppressed or ignored. Said's discussions focus mainly on Asia and North Africa. But the power dynamics he describes can open up ways of thinking about any instance of imperialism. What Said suggests is that for one country to have power over another, it must treat that country *as* other – as at once different from and inferior to itself. And this process of what we might call 'othering' is certainly visible in *She*. As Holly, Vincey and their manservant Job travel to central Africa, we are privy to many assumptions about the exotic, seductive, dangerous nature of central Africa. And the novel is not without the more overt racism which disfigures much writing of its time either. The man who captains the men's boat as they begin their expedition is described as a 'stout swarthy Arab' (52), is named Mahomed and is given few characteristics other than his skin colour and frequent imprecations to Allah. And the Amahagger people who capture Holly and his cohort and bring them to their Queen, are similarly judged and stereotyped immediately, on the basis of their physique and physiognomy:

> They were of a magnificent build, few of them being under six feet in height, and yellowish in colour. Generally their appearance had a good deal in common with the East African Somali, only their hair was not frizzed up, and hung in thick black locks upon their shoulders. Their features were aquiline, and in many cases exceedingly handsome, the teeth being especially regular and beautiful. But notwithstanding their beauty, it struck me that, on the whole, I had never seen a more evil-looking set of faces. There was an aspect of cold and sullen cruelty stamped upon them that revolted me, and which in some cases was almost uncanny in its intensity. (75)

The tone of cool scientific appraisal leads easily from the description of physical type to facial appearance to an imputation of moral characteristics – a move in line at once with general Victorian psychological thinking and its more specific stance towards race.

Racial categorization – mainly in terms of skin colour – has been a feature of European thought since the seventeenth century, but took on new forms in the nineteenth century, as interest grew in the development and identification of biological species. Charles Hamilton Smith's *The Natural History of the Human Species* (1848) must be mentioned here, along with Robert Knox's *The Races of Man* (1850). The assumption behind the establishment of different racial species is that variations in biological types explain differences in culture. And these differences tend to be thought about in hierarchical – and hence *racist* – terms, differences between cultures being read against the standard of the implicitly superior Western norm. Indeed, as Ashcroft et al have argued ' "racism" is not so much a product of the concept of race as the very reason for its existence. Without the underlying desire for hierarchical categorization implicit in racism, "race" would not exist' (Ashcroft 1998, 181). Again, this argument points to the 'interested' nature of the impulse to know. The very project of seeking to know, through differentiating, the races, starts from the point of view of one's 'own' race and the values one attaches to it. This is not to suggest, of course, that all attempts to know someone or something or country are wrong; but that one must always be attentive to the implicit assumptions that are *there* in one's point of departure.

The 'orientalism' of *She* is not confined to simple observations about race and character, but takes on larger symbolic connotations. The matriarchal structures of the Amahagger, in which 'descent is traced only through the line of the mother' (79), are placed in direct contrast with Western systems of patrilineage – 'individuals are as proud of a long and superior female ancestry as we are of our families in Europe' (79). And the *politesse* of middle-class late-Victorian society is juxtaposed with the cruelty of the cannibalistic Amahagger, their savagery a foil to civilized English procedures. As Holly remarks, in a formulation which itself demonstrates that his 'civilized' wit has not left him, 'It is hospitality turned upside down [...]. In our country we entertain a stranger and give him food to eat. Here ye eat him, and are entertained' (101). Daniel Karlin sums the matter up, writing that the Amahagger 'are depicted as a European's racial and sexual nightmare, a demonic cannibalistic matriarchy squatting in the ruins of a lost civilization, sheltering in its tombs and using its desecrated mummies for fuel' (Haggard 1991, xv). It is easy, then, to see the novel as operating through a series of hierarchical oppositions, in which the tribe of central African people is set up – 'othered', we might say – as the bad negative of everything civilized Englishness stands for. We could point out further that its imperialist assumptions are bound up with misogyny. One set of power relations – between the West and its others – is related to another – between men and women. Late-Victorian fears about powerful women feed into and support the 'othering' of the Amahagger.

This is not the whole story, however. For a start, and as Karlin has also pointed out, the 'two Amahagger who have major roles in the book, Billali and Ustane, are sympathetically presented' (xv). Billali, the 'father' of the Amahagger people, is represented as courteous and wise, and Ustane, who marries Leo according to her people's custom by kissing him publicly, is tender and so devoted to her husband that she braves the Queen's wrath to see him once more and is killed by her. But these elements – while important to notice – are not in themselves sufficient to exonerate *She* from accusations that it sets up rather crass and hierarchical oppositions between England and Africa. We might read them, rather, as classic instances of the 'exception that proves the rule'. These characters' remarkable qualities simply endorse the 'fact' that *most* Amahagger are cruel, heartless and savage. In the imperialist context they also point to another of the ways in which such power does its work. In order to have any contact with native cultures, go-between figures, translators and mediators, are required. And in much colonialist literature these are represented as the so-called 'good natives', whose compliance and – so it is imagined – semi-'civilized' qualities, set them apart from the mass, but also allow a point of contact with it.

The character of Dr Aziz in Forster's *A Passage to India* (1924) might be read as one such figure. His education and status enable him to converse with the English ruling classes, who turn on him, however, once he is accused of rape, an accusation which itself arises in part out of a racist fear of oriental passion and cunning. Billali is represented as a similarly exceptional figure in *She*, and one who mediates between the violent hordes and the civilized English travellers. He allows them safe passage as they flee at the end of the book and so, presumably, lives on. Ustane however is not permitted to live. And her death at the hands of the vengeful Queen simultaneously idealizes her as the sacrificial type of female self-abnegation and devotion, and gets the novel out of the unthinkable situation of concluding with the blond Grecian beauty Leo married to a black woman. The goodness of the 'good native' here is itself complicit with 'orientalist' think- ing, keeping intact the fundamental hierarchies and distinctions such thinking upholds. On the other hand the novel's treatment of Africa is more complicated – less black and white – than its most obvious symbolic oppositions would suggest. And its complications can help us reflect further on the question of liter- ature's relationship to empire.

# Anxieties of Empire: Homi Bhabha and hybridity

What emerges when we continue to read the novel is that the attempt to know the central African tribe – and later its white Queen – prompt reflections in our masterful narrator which *don't* simply endorse the superiority of the West, but on the contrary might be said to trouble it. For a start, in making comparisons between his own culture and that of the Amahagger, Horace Holly is obliged to notice similarities as well as differences. Upon witnessing Ustane's claiming of a kiss from Leo, the working-class Job exclaims 'The hussy – well, I never!' (79) – giving voice to the affront such ostensible forwardness offers to English morality. But for the middle-class, educated Holly the marriage customs of the Amahagger tribe, in which a woman chooses her mate through kissing him, and he accepts by returning the embrace, lead to other reflections:

> It is very curious to observe how the customs of mankind on this matter vary in different countries, making morality an affair of latitude, and what is right and proper in one place wrong and improper in another. It must, however, be understood that, as all civilised nations appear to accept it as an axiom that ceremony is the touchstone of morality, there is, even according to our canons, nothing immoral about this Amahagger custom, seeing that the interchange of the embrace answers to our ceremony of marriage, which, as we know, justifies most things. (79–80)

The encounter between cultures here leads not to a hierarchy of moral values, but to a consideration of morality itself. And this starts to seem to Holly a relative rather than absolute affair. Morality is guaranteed in all cultures not by some inner sense of right and wrong but by rites, rituals and ceremonies. What is common across the globe is not morality as such, Holly suggests, but the ceremony that shores it up. And, he implies – in one of those odd lurches from serious reflection to comic innuendo which characterize the book's narration, and perhaps also bespeak some of its anxieties – all sorts of behaviours might occur under the ostensibly 'civilized' cloak of marriage. Holly initially applies here the standards of so-called 'civilized nations' in order to make his relativist argument – but the very notion of what civilization *is* itself becomes uncertain in the process. The Amahagger have ceremonies and customs even if they have no formal laws, and thus, by implication, have no less right to call themselves civilized than do their English observers. And conversely how 'civilized' an English marriage is, is a question left in doubt!

While Holly's tone remains urbane, we are no longer here in the province of the kind of lofty knowledge of the exotic but inferior 'other' described by Said. The direct confrontation with the 'other' seems to bring about the recognition of similarities, rather than a simple sense of cultural superiority. But this isn't exactly a case of acknowledging that we are all essentially the same under the skin – which we might think of as the 'humanist' response to ethnic differences. What happens, rather, is that Holly confronts the fact that all cultures are based on practices, which have no 'essential' meaning in themselves, but which are necessary for the smooth functioning of society. The English and the Amahagger don't share a fundamental moral code, but they do share a belief that morality must be governed by codes. And there seems, then, to be no fixed ground from which to decide which moral code is the best.

This reading of Holly's reflections on English and Amahagger culture can prompt us to further theoretical reflections of our own on literature's relationship to imperialism. Said, as we have seen, suggests that there is a tyrannical one-way encounter between West and East, in which the former imperiously and knowledgeably objectifies the latter, setting itself up as normal and natural in contrast with its alien and exotic other. But what Haggard seems to show us is a more troublesome interaction in which the encounter with 'the other' leads also to reflections upon one's own culture, which denaturalize it and make explicit and legible its own workings and implicit assumptions. The post-colonial theorist Homi Bhabha, writing after and partly in response to Edward Said, has described these more anxious and unsettling aspects of the imperial or colonial encounter. Writing in a rich and complex language, redolent of the muddled-up-ness it seeks to capture, Bhabha uses words such as 'ambivalence', 'mimicry' and 'hybridity' to describe complicated, mixed, in-between colonizer/colonized relationships, which don't quite follow the pattern of hygienic and dispassionate intellectual mastery posited by Said. 'Hybridity' is, as Robert Young (1995) has pointed out, a term initially borrowed from a racist language to describe people of 'mixed race'. But Bhabha appropriates it to describe a more intellectual and experiential 'miscegenation' (originally a racist term used to describe the mixing of blood in interracial relationships) which is disclosed in cross-cultural meetings between the imperialist West and its others.

Hybridity in this sense emerges through the need not only to establish differences but also to make connections – to translate and to mediate between one culture and another. In imperialist and colonial confrontations, this need arises from the desire to master and impose one's own systems of thought and cultural practices upon a native people. In order to do this, those systems have to be explained and translated into comprehensible terms. But the very act of translation thus brings Western practices into an intimate relationship with the culture they are supposed simply to dominate, subjecting them to *its* terms. In missionary work in India, for example, the practice of baptism was often 'translated' as regeneration or second birth – what happens in the Brahman rite of passage. In order to make the Western, Christian practice comprehensible, it becomes likened precisely to that which it seeks to supplant. As Bhabha puts it in his famously rebarbative prose 'hybridity is a problematic of colonial representation and individuation that reverses the effects of the colonialist disavowal, so that other "denied" knowledges enter upon the dominant discourse and estrange the basis of its authority' (1994, 115). In other words: in order to impose one's superior knowledge and language upon another, the other's knowledge has to be conjured with and *ac*knowledged, however grudgingly – the other's words have to be spoken. In this process, the supposed superiority of the imperialist's mastery falters, as he betrays the fact that his supposedly masterful language and ideas can quite easily be explained in those of another, supposedly simpler or inferior, culture. This culture starts, then, to seem neither so different nor so simple after all.

Bhabha takes up Said's model of orientalist dominance then, and suggests a less easy, more anxious quality to the imperialist's relationship with those over whom he holds sway. He uses the Freudian word 'ambivalence' to describe the unease produced by such encounters (1994, 85). Ambivalence is not, in this psychoanalytic sense, a lukewarm or undecided sentiment, but a profound tornness – love and hate, need and rejection at the same time. In order to define his own identity and values, the Westerner does so against the 'other' whom s/he encounters. As Said has said, this seems to result in a stereotyping and fixing of the other's 'identity'. But if that identity is necessary to the assertion of Western values and qualities, then it cannot *simply* be rejected, but must also be sustained and cherished in its difference. To put it more baldly, an imperialist or a colonizer can only exist if there is a people to be ruled or colonized. And the existence of that people is therefore not something secondary or dismissable but is – uneasily – essential and necessary, and indeed prior to the existence of the colonizer, who nevertheless wants to imagine himself as 'first'.

In some ways, these complex, hybrid, ambivalent kinds of relationship and feeling can be seen at work when Holly attempts to relate English and Amahagger culture in the passage from *she* quoted above (79–80). The distinction between 'good' and 'bad' natives we've already discussed can also be understood symbolically as a playing out of the Westerners' simultaneous dependency on and fear of their Amahagger captors. And the comparison of marriage rights seems to lead to a hybrid model of cultural relations. There are differences between the cultures, but similarities too, and those similarities – the emphasis upon ritual and ceremony – point up the workings of the bedrock of the English family, showing it to be a matter of convention and formula, rather than something natural or right. The English sense of what is 'natural', then, is itself revealed as a product of social and cultural codes. But what we *don't* glimpse in this scene is any of the anxiety Bhabha attributes to such moments of uneasy (and often – though not here – unconscious) realization. Holly seems happy to accept the moral and cultural relativism in which his compare and contrast exercise results. On the other hand, the passage certainly shores up other power relations – this time those of class. The working-class Job is kept firmly in his place through the rather stereotypical depiction of his comic outrage at Amahagger female forwardness, while Holly's more easy-going stance is implicitly attributed to his superior wisdom and middle-class 'liberal' education. Two things emerge from this. First, just as it is absurd to sum up a variegated body of people as 'Orientals' or even to suggest that a single ethnic group is homogenous, so it is nonsensical to assume that the Western 'imperialists' constitute a single body. And indeed the disclosure of the workings of class in this scene might well be understood as a further effect of hybridity, the reflections on another culture revealing once again but in a different way the hidden structures of one's own. Second, when we translate terms from post-colonial theory into the language of literary criticism, we must never forget that it *is* literature we are discussing. To expect 'ambivalence' or unease from Holly is to treat him as a psychologically fleshed-out human being, whereas Holly, Billali and Job are, of course, fictional characters, conjured by Haggard.

This does not mean, however, that we must abandon Bhabha's ideas of ambivalence and hybridity when talking about literature – but rather that simply to see them as something experienced by literary characters would be wrong. In fact, there are many ways in which we might want to think about literature *itself* as a site of ambivalence and as a hybrid phenomenon. If hybridity emerges in the act of explaining and mediating one's own cultural terms to another, repeating and representing them in other terms – well then, literature is always engaged in such repetition, representation and mediation. What happens in the imperial or colonial encounter with other cultures is itself, then, a repetition of what literature already does. Literature repeats what are taken as the norms and givens of a culture, rendering them through a selective set of codes and clues – Job's working-class Norfolk accent, Leo's easy, public-school slang, the accoutrements these characters carry, and so on – and showing in the process how culture itself operates through codes and shibboleths. We talked in chapter 2 about literature's capacity to 'defamiliarize' – to make the world strange to us through its rendering of it. Literature, we might now say, makes the familiar *foreign*, even while it makes the foreign and distant known to or knowable by us.

## Empires of the imagination

But literature, of course, does not have to rest with a realistic representation of the known and the familiar. The romance tale *She* takes an ever more fantastical course, moving us beyond the furthest reaches of the known world and into the realm of mysterious Kôr and its two-thousand-year-old Empress – who turns out, of course, to be the very same woman who slew Leo's ancient forefather, Kallikrates. Kôr is an eerie place, with complex networks of caves containing the mummified dead, and surrounded by the colossal ruins of a lost civilization. And it is here that Holly experiences his most ambivalent feelings. Many of these take a quite easily recognizable form, even while they are prompted by outlandish happenings. He is at once enraptured and appalled by the cruel beauty of Ayesha (as She is called); and his sight of the preserved body of the dead Kallikrates, who could be Leo's twin, causes him to 'shrink back terrified' for, as he says, 'the sight was an uncanny one' (211).

Perhaps more uncanny than these strange but generically familiar Gothic occurrences ('I was getting used to eerie sensations by this time' says Holly at one point (121)) are the interactions and conversations he has with the ancient but youthful-looking Ayesha, witnessing how she governs her subjects, filling her in on two millennia of world history and describing his own culture to her. It is here that odd similarities and parallels emerge between the workings of Western imperialism and the empire of the cruel but compelling Ayesha. For a start, there is a resemblance, unremarked by Holly but legible to the reader, between the effect of his use of guns upon the Amahagger, who view his shooting of wild animals as 'a very high-class manifestation of witchcraft' (119) and Holly's own response to She's telepathic powers, crying out that they must be 'magic'. She corrects him, saying that 'it is no magic; that is a fiction of ignorance. There is no such thing as magic, though there is such a thing as a knowledge of the secrets of Nature' (140).

The power of techno-scientific advances to subdue through their mystery is a recurrent feature of imperial and colonial domination. When the mid-sixteenth-century astronomer, mathematician, ethnographer and translator Thomas Harriot was left at an English colony in Virginia by Sir Walter Raleigh in 1586, for example, part of his task was to bring 'civilization' to the Native Americans (then called Indians). He wrote a report on his experiences, recording how everyday English instruments, such as guns, mathematical instruments, clocks, books and indeed writing, were seen by these people as 'rather the works of gods than of men'. Harriot's testimony implies that the English used these ostensibly god-like powers to impose English beliefs in a *Christian* God on the 'natives', and to gain power over them. The twentieth-century New Historicist theorist Stephen Greenblatt, in an essay called 'Invisible Bullets', reads this sixteenth-century account alongside Shakespeare's *Henry V*, to show that the explicit workings of power described in the former are also manifest in the latter (Greenblatt 1988). Greenblatt's work takes a slightly different approach to the contexualizing of literature from the ones we discussed in chapter 4. New Historicists look at the 'textuality of history' as well as the 'historicity of texts', reading contemporary non-literary documents alongside works of literature, in order to point out similarities in the two, which they link to the ways in which power could always be said to be at work in society (Veeser 1994, 20). Taking these insights into the workings of power back to our late-nineteenth-century imperial context, we can see that Ayesha's comments reveal two things. First, religion has an ideological function, and can be used in the service of power. And second, techniques of power are once again intertwined with knowledge. Ayesha, too, unveils and demystifies the intertwining of power and knowledge in imperialism. It is not only that knowing 'the secrets of Nature' gives one specific abilities, but also more generally that authority lies in having a knowledge others don't possess. But in this instance it is the 'exotic' Egyptian empress who has the knowledge, and, furthermore, the capacity to reflect on the power that knowledge gives, unveiling its workings, even as she keeps secret the specific nature of her knowledge.

Ayesha is articulate about many of the ways in which power does its work. Summarily condemning to torture and death the Amahagger who disobeyed her orders, she explains to Holly, who has pleaded for clemency, that to show mercy would be to relinquish her power. 'My empire', she says, 'is of the imagination' (161). She, like imperialists and tyrants both ancient and modern, is aware of the power of images and spectacles to magnify actual violence, and create a mystique more compelling than the simple deployment of forces. (Shakespeare's *Henry V*, with its emphases on the rhetoric and spectacle of kingly power, could also be said to do this.) And again what is remarkable and sinister here is the way in which She unveils the very means through which power operates – an unveiling which nevertheless does not take us to a single truth, but rather to the power of ideas, images and fictions. It is in these, she suggests, that power lies.

Ayesha is able to offer this lofty view of power because of her longevity – she has lived through the rise and fall of numerous civilizations, and can take the long view of religions too, remarking that 'the religions come and the religions pass, and the civilizations come and pass, and naught endures but the world and human nature' (174). Judaism, Christianity and Islam are, for her, but different ways in which humans seek to banish 'terror for the end'. Religion, she suggests, is 'but a subtler form of selfishness' (174). And, employing an agnostic materialism which, as Holly points out, can also be 'heard in the nineteenth century, and in other places than the caves of Kôr', she exclaims: 'Ah! if man would but see that hope is from within and not from without – that he himself must work out his own salvation! He is there, and within him is the breath of life' (174). What Ayesha is taking on here is the way in which people validate and vindicate their actions by appealing to an exterior ideal. Such justifications certainly underpinned imperialist expansion as well as colonialist occupation – the idea that Christian truth, or greater wisdom and enlightenment, were selflessly being brought to the dark, pagan parts of the globe covered over the fact that these parts of the earth had materials and goods needed by the West.

Ayesha seems, then, from within the bounds of an imperialist romance, to offer a wholesale debunking of the imperialist
enterprise – even while she, herself, is keen to expand her
empire. But she is able to do this in part because she is such an
improbable fiction. Haggard can give her heretical utterances
and seditious insights into empire, precisely because she is so
exotically 'other'. Her extraordinary beauty and her improbable
life-span put her outside the conventions and restrictions that
would have been placed on the speech and thought even of a
liberally educated late Victorian man such as Horace Holly. That
she dies at the end of the novel, burned by the flames in which
she seeks to renew her life once more, can be read as an ideological insurance policy: a bid to close down and condemn the
voice which has spoken so eloquently through the book's pages,
and continues to haunt its readers after it has been put down.

Two theoretical points can be made here. First, returning to
Homi Bhabha, we can suggest that the anxiety her pronounce-
ments produce in Horace Holly (and may well have caused in a
late Victorian reader too) are a function at once of her mysterious 'otherness' and the strange *similarities* between what she says
about her own empire and those of the British Empire. It is this
mixture of difference and sameness that, for Bhabha, produces
the unsettling experience of ambivalence, and the mixed-up
phenomenon of hybridity. As we see in *She* these moments are
produced through cross-cultural conversations, in which each
party tries to convey and 'translate' their own view-point to the
other. And in Holly's case, this conversation results in his own
cultural assumptions being revealed and challenged.

Second, Ayesha's disclosure of the workings of the 'Empire
of Imagination' demonstrates how tied up imperial and colonial
power are *with* imagination, and with related things such as literature, theatre and writing. It is through the theatrical slaughter
of a few troublesome members of the Amahagger that her reign
of terror is enforced. She does not have a great army herself, but

is able to convey her might through the occasional, highly visible, act of power, which by virtue of its visibility has a reach far beyond the lives of those whom it immediately destroys. And literature, by doubling up acts of power such as this through its representation of them, is able to make visible its workings, even while demonstrating the forcefully fictive aspects of power itself. There are many twentieth and twenty-first-century instances of power being used in this way, to produce 'shock and awe' in less technologically advanced nations. You will, I'm sure, be able to think of examples yourself. In terms of the 'new forms of imperialism' we read McClintock discussing at the start of this chapter, we might also think about the ways in which 'new media' and technologies such as the internet or Twitter have the capacity to spread images and sound-bites swiftly round the world, changing what might have been a local event into something which has the power to affect countries and people thousands of miles away.

This reflection on the *power* of literature and other media can lead us to further theoretical reflections too on literature's relationship to the empires and powers it represents. Homi Bhabha also has things to say about this, and we can return to *She* to elaborate them further. He points to a scene which happens repeatedly in both historical and fictional literature about empire and colonialism: 'it is the scenario, played out in the wild and worldless wastes of colonial India, Africa, the Caribbean, of the sudden, fortuitous discovery of the English book' (1994, 102). In the instances he describes – from accounts by missionaries, Joseph Conrad's *The Heart of Darkness* and an essay by V. S. Naipaul – an English book (in the first case the Bible) is found in the midst of a foreign country. Its foreign location makes it seem like the very essence of Englishness – but its 'translation' into a strange place, and in some cases the fact that it is 'misread' – which is to say approached by native peoples on their own terms – make it also strange. It appears as so superlatively English precisely because of the way in which it is deracinated, and read through other eyes. Bhabha says that the repeated 'scene' he identifies in empire literature is what 'triumphantly *inaugurates* a literature of empire' (102). And I think we are to understand that phrase 'literature of empire' in two ways: both as literature *about* empire, but also in terms of the imperious power that literature can have, for good or ill.

As we have said before in this book, the fact of writing – its very material existence – along with the act of reading which it calls up, has great power. It has the power to summon us imaginatively and intellectually, to call us to action, to expose fictions and ideologies at work in the world and to unsettle us by disturbing our sense of what the world is, making us see it with new eyes. Rider Haggard's *She* has the power to do this. Generations of readers have attested to this. The psychoanalysts Freud and Jung both wrote about it, and the writer Elizabeth Bowen, herself part of a colonial power as a member of the Anglo-Irish ascendancy, said of it in a radio broadcast fifty years after its publication:

> This book *She* is for me historic – it stands for the first totally violent impact I ever received from print. After *She* print was to fill me with apprehension. I was prepared to handle any book like a bomb. (Bowen 1999, 250)

She goes on to link its power explicitly with writing:

> Writing – that creaking, pedantic, obtrusive, arch, prudish, opaque overworded *writing* ... what it could do! That was the revelation; that was the power in the cave. The power whose inequality dear Holly laments at the opening of every passage. The power of the pen. The inventive pen. (250)

*She* itself has a moment which attests to this power. In the later part of the novel, when Holly has travelled to 'mysterious Kôr' he (like the reader at the start of the novel) encounters an inscription in 'extraordinary characters' unfamiliar and unintelligible to him (163). And the encounter gives rise to precisely the kind of vertiginously uneasy feeling that he is so blithely able to hold off in his meetings with the Amahagger. The script – which Ayesha translates for him – was written by the last survivor of the city of Kôr, amongst whose ancient ruins she dwells with her mute servants. She testifies that the inscription has been there throughout her own two thousand years of life. And it tells how the city ruled the world and traded with it for 'four thousand eight hundred and three' years before it fell to the ravages of a plague, all its 'mighty works' destroyed and left 'for the wolf and the owl and the wild swan, and the barbarian who comes after' (164). Holly says 'I gave a sigh of astonishment – the utter desolation depicted in this rude scrawl was so overpowering'. Its power is twofold. It at once prompts – in Holly, the subject of imperial England as well as in his reader – thoughts about the weakness of the mightiest power in the face of time, disease and other accidents. And it points to the mightier power of writing, which has the capacity to outlast all human power, and, while there is still a single reader left, to communicate across vast temporal and historical reaches, unsettling and dislocating the most apparently secure of beliefs.

*She*, with its fascination with all kinds of foreign writings, allows us to see, then, the intimate foreignness of writing *itself*, and to feel the strange ways in which literature can dislodge our own fixed sense of our identities, personal but also cultural and ethnic. Reading *She*'s writing closely we might point out here that Rider Haggard gives the Amahagger a name which in its four syllables seems to echo his own, and in which most of his surname is inscribed. The 'editor' punctiliously furnishes us with a hybrid etymology for the tribal name, 'ama' being a Zulu word signifying 'people' and 'hagger' the Arabic for stone (165). On the one hand Haggard seems to monumentalize his own name here, writing it into the book covertly, as though to stamp his authority on it. On the other hand, he thereby links himself with this tribe, the most 'foreign' and 'othered' people in his book. And what we share, it is implied, is not a common spirit, but something at once stranger and more intimate – rhythms and letters, little word-sherds, more matter and stone than spirit, more primal than sense – shapes and sounds meaningless in themselves but necessary to all meaning. Writing's empire comes down to the smallest things – to letters and stones, pen and paper, keypads and screens – and yet it has the power to create and to destroy, to enable the functioning of empires and colonies and to expose their workings. Which of these it does depends in great part on how it is read. Post-colonial theorists such as Bhabha encourage us to read closely, to the letter, in order to expose the power that letters have and to put it to better uses, or to experience and endorse the witness writing's more mute or marginalized voices bear. Their theoretical analyses can be read as an injunction that each of us read as though we were the last person on earth, the last witness, as though the whole globe and its future depended upon us. This injunction, while it is of the utmost seriousness, needn't preclude pleasure or humour. *She* is punctuated by awful jokes and moments of bathos which bring us crashing down to earth. After some grand metaphysical reflections on Life, its meaning and its shortness, Holly says that he 'at last managed to get to sleep, a fact for which anybody who reads this narrative, if anybody ever does, may very probably be thankful' (112). Laughter can be a good response to tyranny, and being brought down to earth can remind us of the earth that we share. Haggard's writing does this – and reminds us of writing's earthy and earthly power always to do so.

# Coda: Theory's futures

Winston Smith, covertly writing a diary in the nightmarish totalitarian regime which Orwell conjures in *Nineteen Eighty-Four*, wonders what – and whether – the future could be without writing.

> How could you make appeal to the future when not a trace of you, not even an anonymous word scribbled on a piece of paper, could physically survive? (Orwell, 1987, 29)

Writing for Winston is the best, perhaps the only, form of resistance to a regime which stills time to a perpetual present, and controls language, paring it down and taking all the 'give' out of it. Throughout our readings in this *Beginner's Guide* we have repeatedly found that it is the give, the grace and also the recalcitrance of specific and singular works of literature, which 'make appeal' to the future. And we have also seen how readings attempt to respond – fallibly, partially, but singularly – to that appeal.

The role of 'literary theory' within this dynamic of appeal and response is a strange one. As we saw in the second chapter, and continued to discover in new ways throughout, literature seems to exist as the promise of always-singular encounters, which are marked by the date and signature of their inscription, and recognized in a particular and idiomatic moment of reading. Throughout this book, no *general* theory of literature or of reading has seemed possible. And yet it was only through a recurrent putting of that fact to the test that the singularity of literature, repeatedly and differently, quirkily or comically, poetically or prosaically, shone through. And it did so precisely because of the ways in which it resisted any theoretical attempt to master it. Not to theorize about literature at all would be simply to repeat its own words, in a stammering tautology which would keep us in a perpetual present. To offer a general theory of literature, on the other hand, would be to quell literature under a totalitarian regime and leave it nothing to give. Theory exists in a tension between its aspirations to a lucid generality and its recognition that it is implicated in, and summoned by, the literary force-fields it wants to stand outside. It is this tension which I have tried to remain true to throughout this book.

In a paper called 'The Resistance to Theory', which surveys the past of literary theory and looks to its future, Paul de Man suggests that it is this tension within theory that assures its passage into a future. He writes that 'literary theory is not in danger of going under; it cannot help but flourish, and the more it is resisted, the more it flourishes, since the language that it speaks is the language of self-resistance' (20). Theory for de Man lives on as an always-ruined project, flourishing precisely through its failure to theorize everything. It is this lack of mastery within it that allows theory itself to be read, as we have been reading it in this book, eliciting insights from it and seeing also its blindness. And reading theory therefore opens up new possibilities both for theory and for reading.

Since de Man wrote his essay literary theory has continued to 'flourish'. We could recount this in terms of a proliferation of new –isms, schools and –ologies and posts- treating 'pseudo-identities, labels, or slogans as little wooden horses in a merry-go-round where New Criticism, structuralism, post-structuralism, new socio-historicism, and then again formalism, nonformalism, and so on would follow one another', to quote

Derrida's riff on this kind of approach (Derrida 1990, 78). Names and labels can be helpful in allowing us to get a handle on things. And so I'll just refer here to theories which go by the names of 'presentism', of the 'new aestheticism', of the 'new geography' and indeed of 'post-theory', towards the reading of which the recommendations in the 'further reading' section point.

More generally and perhaps more interestingly, theory has emerged in critical writing in more local, provisional, less masterful ways over the last few decades. The 'queer theorist' Eve Sedgwick talks in this regard helpfully of 'weak theory': she suggests, that 'there are important phenomenological and theoretical tasks that can be accomplished only through local theories and nonce taxonomies' (Sedgwick 2003, 145). For Sedgwick, this kind of provisional or local theory, more or less made up for the occasion like a nonce-word, opens up a new range of ways of talking about *feeling*, or what she calls in psychoanalytic terminology 'affect', in relation to literature. By this she does not mean just a single feeling, such as pleasure, but a nuanced range of them, a new vocabulary for talking at once rigorously and flexibly about literary response. Her intention is not to give up either on thinking or on abstraction – but to recognize that there are *degrees* of abstraction, and that, since no theory *can* ever justify itself absolutely, it would be as well to recognize that. The kind of theory on the fly that Sedgwick advocates – a theory which strives for rigour, but acknowledges its own provisional and contingent nature – can be seen in recent literary-theoretical work that has turned to phenomena we don't necessarily think of as *essential* components of literature – to ghosts, mutants, secrets or stupidity, for example. That's not to suggest that the 'big questions' are forgotten, however. Literary theorists have also turned their attention to terrorism, to trauma and to religion. Suggestions for where to find all these possibilities are given in the 'further reading'.

As I discussed in my introduction, theory first emerged, as the hybrid, heterogeneous creature that it is, mainly in universities. It has been instituted as a 'discipline' there and has given rise to courses and whole degree programmes within the institution of the university at large. You may well be reading this book because you are taking such a course. But if theory flourishes through its own internal resistance and impossibility then this puts it in a strange position vis-à-vis what Graham Allen has called 'the techno-scientific, instrumentalist and bureaucratic discourses and powers that currently dominate the university' (2006, 1). Its own venturesome essays, speculations, provocations, its flourishing, singular failures and the fact that it not only proposes theories of reading but needs to be read, seems to resist assimilation into a model of education in which teaching 'aims and objectives' and 'what students will have learned from this course' have to be laid out before any reading has begun. If theory necessarily fails in some way, then we might wonder what it would mean to pass – or fail – a course on literary theory that was set up in terms of assured and measurable outcomes. Such a model of success or failure seems to close down the futures that writing, reading and theory together strive to keep open. Some of the most exciting recent developments in literary theory have been those which address themselves to this situation, exploring the role of literature, of theory and of thought in teaching and learning today. The question of how to make room in the university for kinds of thinking which take the risk of reading, and give up on the absolute security which would be able to predict its own outcomes, are at issue in all of these. Again, they're mentioned in the further reading.

That is not to suggest that 'theory' is *confined* to educational institutions, however. Indeed its capacity to challenge and put those institutions to question suggests that it never fully belongs to them. And, in so far as literary theory, like literature itself, can always be reduced to a set of methods, surveys of –isms and check-lists of key points by the requirements of universities and schools, we might suggest that one of its best hopes for continual flourishing will be outside the university.

Indeed theory's 'futures' lie wherever it is read carefully, thoughtfully, inventively and with a view to the surprises it might always have in store. Just as Althusser suggests that our best hope of moving on is to go back and read Marx, slowly and attentively, so we might suggest that literary theory's futures lie in the fact that *as* writings, the body of texts which make up its canon and corpus can themselves be read and reread, into the future. For this reason, its futures don't simply lie in new schools and movements – in *further* reading understood as simply reading new things. They also lie in rereading – and in the readers, such as you and me, who undertake that reading.

# Further reading

## Chapter 1

Baldick, Chris. 1983. *The Social Mission of English Studies 1848–1932*. Oxford, Oxford University Press. A detailed and lucid account of the history of English studies, moving from Matthew Arnold to I. A. Richards, T. S. Eliot and the Leavises.

Barry, Peter. 2009. *Beginning Theory*. 3rd edn. Manchester, Manchester University Press. Introduces theory through accounts of a series of movements and schools. Offers lists of what particular theorists 'do'.

Bennett, Andrew and Nicholas Royle. 2009. *An Introduction to Literature, Criticism and Theory*. 4th edn. Harlow, Pearson Longman. A brilliant, lively introduction to literature and its theories, which really makes literature and theory resonate productively together.

Derrida, Jacques. 1990. 'Some Statements and Truisms about Neologisms, Newisms, Postisms, Parasitisms, and Other Small Seismisms', in *The States of "Theory"*, ed. David Carroll. New York, Columbia University Press. A witty criticism of the approach to theory which sees it as a series of movements, schools and –isms, and an argument for *reading* theory for its inventive possibilities.

Graff, Gerald. 1987. *Professing Literature: An Institutional History*. Chicago, Chicago University Press. Explores the development of the study of English literature and theories of literature in the United States from the nineteenth century onwards.

# Chapter 2

Attridge, Derek. *Peculiar Language: Literature as Difference from the Renaissance to Joyce*. Routledge, 1988. A witty, intelligent and informative book, which covers a broad historical sweep in impressive and lucid detail.

Beaumont Bissell, Elizabeth, ed. 2002. *The Question of Literature: The Place of the Literary in Contemporary Theory*. Manchester, Manchester University Press. Collects a range of thoughtful and often dazzling essays, which demonstrate that the 'question of literature' still flourishes productively in the twenty-first century.

Clark, Timothy. 1992. *Derrida, Heidegger, Blanchot: Sources of Derrida's Notion and Practice of Literature*. Cambridge, Cambridge University Press. Not an easy book, but the difficulty lies in the thinking, not in the writing, which is lucid, and exemplifies 'deconstructive' arguments about literature through readings of a poem.

Lentricchia, Frank and Andrew du Bois. 2003. *Close Reading: The Reader*. Durham NC, Duke University Press. A collection of 'New Critical' essays and later work which develops out of 'close reading'.

Page, N. 1984. *The Language of Literature*. Casebook series, Macmillan. Collects a number of essays on 'literariness'.

Tambling, Jeremy. 1998. *What is Literary Language?* Open University Press. A short and helpful introduction to discussions about 'literariness'.

# Chapter 3

Attridge, Derek. 2004. *J. M. Coetzee and the Ethics of Reading: Literature in the Event*. Chicago, University of Chicago Press. A reflection on and an exemplification of what reading ethically might look like.

Barthes, Roland. 1993. *A Barthes Reader*, ed. Susan Sontag. London, Vintage. A collection of this witty, stimulating and provocative writer's work.

Bennett, Andrew, ed. 1995. *Readers and Reading*. London, Longman. A collection of theories of reading and response, ranging widely from Wolfgang Iser to Shoshana Felman to Yves Bonnefoy. The introduction is very lucid and helpful.

Biriotti, Maurice, ed. 1993. *What is an Author?* Manchester, Manchester University Press. See especially Gayatri Spivak's 'Reading *The Satanic Verses*' – an exploration of the fatwah declared against Rushdie in the context of discussions about the role of the author and authorial responsibility.

Derrida, Jacques. 1998. *A Derrida Reader*. Ed. Peggy Kamuf. Columbia, Columbia University Press. A collection of Derrida's writings. The essay 'Signature Event Context' is a good place to start, and offers a really cogent account of what is necessary for there to be meaning and communication.

Empson, William. 1995. *Seven Types of Ambiguity*. Harmondsworth, Penguin. A reprint of Empson's 1930 *tour de force*, which reads more 'closely' than many of his contemporaries. T. S. Eliot called it the 'lemon squeezer' school of criticism, but it offers an interesting and often dazzling example of 'New Critical' reading methods going beyond themselves.

Foucault, Michel. 1977. 'What is an author?' in *Language, Counter-Memory, Practice: Selected Essays and Interviews*, ed. by Donald F. Bouchard, trans. by Bouchard and Sherry Simon. Ithaca, Cornell University Press. Written in (critical) response to Barthes's 'The Death of the Author', Foucault's essay argues that we should explore the ways in which the *idea* of the author functions at specific historical moments.

Royle, Nicholas, ed. 2000. *Deconstructions: A User's Guide*. Basingstoke, Palgrave. A collection of 'singular' essays. In this context, see especially Rodolphe Gasche's discussion of the relationship between 'Deconstruction and Hermenuetics', and Peggy Kamuf on 'Deconstruction and Love'. All the essays offer helpful ways to think about deconstruction.

# Chapter 4

Bate, Jonathan. 1991. *Romantic Ecology: Wordsworth and the Environmental Tradition*. London, Routledge

Eagleton, Terry. 1990. *The Ideology of the Aesthetic*. Oxford, Blackwell. A study of the various notions of 'ideology' – and their relationship to art and literature – since Marx.

Gallagher, Catherine and Stephen Greenblatt. 2000. *Practicing the New Historicism*. Chicago, Chicago University Press. New Historicism represents another way of thinking about texts in relationship to their 'contexts'. It discusses history as always textual, and texts as always historical.

Greenblatt, Stephen. 1991. *Shakespearian Negotiations: The Circulation of Social Energy in Renaissance England*. California, California University Press. Greenblatt is the prime mover in 'New Historicism'. See especially the essay on 'Fiction and Friction'. I discuss another of Greenblatt's essays in chapter 7 of this Beginner's Guide.

Mulhern, Francis, ed. 1992. *Contemporary Marxist Literary Criticism*. London, Longman. Contains many important essays and has an excellent introduction.

# Chapter 5

Bersani, Leo. 1976. *A Future for Astyanax: Character and Desire in Literature*. Boston, Little Brown. A forceful and brilliant discussion of the relationships between the representation of character in literature, and desire.

Ellman, Maud, ed. 1994. *Psychoanalytic Literary Criticism*. Harlow, Longman. Contains literary criticism which works with Freud's and Lacan's ideas.

Felman, Shoshana, ed. 1982. *Literature and Psychoanalysis – The Question of Reading*. Baltimore, Johns Hopkins University Press. Felman's own essay in this collection 'Turning the Screw of Interpretation' is a masterful, pleasurable and tormenting account of the relationship between reading and desire, with reference to Henry James's short story 'The Turn of the Screw'. This collection also contains an essay by Lacan on Hamlet.

Hall, Donald E. 2003. *Queer Theories*. Basingstoke, Palgrave Macmillan. A good overview.

Sedgwick, Eve. 1991. *Epistemology of the Closet*. Hemel Hempstead, Harvester Wheatsheaf. A deserved classic of queer readings of literature and identity. The 'axiomatics' section at the start lays down with incisive wit some of the important principles of queer theory.

# Chapter 6

Cixous, Hélène. 1998. *Stigmata: Escaping Texts*, trans. Eric Prenowitz. London, Routledge. An inspiring collection of Cixous's more recent writing.

Elam, Diane. 1994. *Feminism and Deconstruction: Ms en Abîme*. London, Routledge. A thoughtful, open and engagingly written examination of feminism and its continued importance as a movement at the end of the twentieth century

Mitchell, Juliet and Jacqueline Rose. 1982. *Feminine sexuality: Jacques Lacan and the école freudienne*, trans. Jacqueline Rose. Basingstoke, Macmillan. A collection of important but difficult essays by Jacques Lacan on femininity, along with two excellent introductory essays.

Moi, Toril. 1985. *Sexual/Textual Politics: Feminist Literary Theory*. London, Routledge. A very good, clear, and probingly critical account of feminist theory from its early days through to the writing of Julia Kristeva.

Warhol, Robyn R. and Diane Price Herndl, eds. 1997. *Feminism: An Anthology of Literary Theory and Criticism*. Rev'd edn. London, Macmillan. An anthology packed with a good span of feminist theory and criticism.

# Chapter 7

Ashcroft, Bill, Gareth Griffiths and Helen Tiffin, eds. *The Post-Colonial Studies Reader*. London, Routledge. A wide-ranging collection of important essays.

Boehmer, Elleke. 2002. *Empire, the national, and the postcolonial, 1890–1920: Resistance in interaction*. Oxford, OUP. A precise, informed and illuminating study, which offers nuanced re-readings of the relationship between modernist literature and empire.

Harrison, Nicholas. 2003. *Postcolonial Criticism: History, Theory and the Work of Fiction*. Cambridge, Polity Press. An original account, which offers clear arguments.

Loomba, Ania. 1998. *Colonialism: Post/Colonialism*. London, Routledge. An excellent introductory work.

Nero, Brian. 2003. *Race*. Basingstoke, Palgrave Macmillan. A good, up-to-date discussion of the notion of race and its implications.

# Coda

## Presentism

Hawkes, Terence. 2002. *Shakespeare in the Present*. London, Routledge

Wells, Robin Headlam. 2000. 'Historicism and "Presentism" in Early Modern Studies', pp. 37–60 in *The Cambridge Quarterly*, vol 29, no 1

## New Aestheticism

Armstrong, Isobel. 2000. *The Radical Aesthetic*. Oxford, Oxford University Press

Joughin, John and Simon Malpas, eds. 2003. *The New Aestheticism*. Manchester, Manchester University Press

## The New Geography

Murphet, Julian. 1999. 'Grounding Theory: Literary Theory and the New Geography' in *Post-Theory: New Directions in Criticism*, ed. by Martin McQuillan et al, Edinburgh, Edinburgh University Press

## Post-theory

See above, plus

Payne, Michael and John Schad. ed. 2003. *Life. After. Theory*. London, Continuum

## The University

Allen, Graham, ed. 2006. 'The Pupils of the University' in *Parallax*, vol 40, July–September

Miller, J. Hills. 1999. *Black Holes/J. Hillis Miller; or Boustrophedonic Reading*. Stanford, Stanford University Press

Readings, Bill. 1994. *The University in Ruins*. Cambridge MA, Harvard University Press

## Other possibilities

Bennett, Andrew and Royle, Nicholas. 2009. *An Introduction to Literature, Criticism and Theory*. 4th edn. Harlow, Pearson Longman. Offers accounts of mutants, ghosts, secrets and war – amongst much else.

Caruth, Cathy. 1996. *Unclaimed Experience: Trauma, Narrative and History*. Baltimore, Johns Hopkins University Press

Derrida, Jacques and Gianni Vattimo, eds. 1998. *Religion*. Cambridge, Polity

Gubar, Susan. 2003. *Poetry After Auschwitz: Remembering what one never knew*. Bloomington, Indiana University Press

Ronell, Avitall. 2002. *Stupidity*. Urbana, University of Illinois Press

# Bibliography of literary works

Bowen, E. 1999. *The Little Girls*. London, Vintage

Carroll, L. 1970. *Alice's Adventures in Wonderland* in *The Annotated Alice*, ed. M. Gardner. Harmondsworth, Penguin

Conrad, J. 1982. 'Author's Note' in *'Twixt Land and Sea*. Harmondsworth, Penguin

——1983–2007. *The Collected Letters of Joseph Conrad*, 8 vols, eds. F. R. Karl and L. Davies. Cambridge, Cambridge University Press

——2007. 'The Secret Sharer' in *The Nigger of the 'Narcissus' and Other Stories*, ed. A. H. Simmons & J. H. Stape. London, Penguin

Dickens, C. 1854. 'On Strike' in *Household Words*, 8: 203, 553–9

——1965–2001. *The Pilgrim Edition of the Letters of Charles Dickens*, ed. M. House *et al*, 11 vols. Oxford, Clarendon Press

——2003. *Hard Times: For These Times*, ed. Kate Flint. London, Penguin

Duffy, C. A. 13 June 2009. 'Politics' in *The Guardian*

Eliot, G. 1985. *Adam Bede*, ed. S. Gill. Harmondsworth, Penguin

Eliot, T. S. 1969. *The Complete Poems and Plays of T. S. Eliot*. London, Faber

Forster, E. M. 1979. *A Passage to India*, ed. O. Stallybrass. Harmondsworth, Penguin

Gaskell, E. 1998. *Mary Barton*, ed. E. Wright. Oxford, Oxford University Press

Goethe, J. W. 2005. *Faust: Part One*, trans. D. Constantine. London, Penguin

Haggard, H. R. 1991. *She*, ed. D. Karlin. Oxford, Oxford University Press

Hopkins, G. M. 2002. *The Major Works*, ed. C. Phillips. Oxford, Oxford University Press

Keats, J. 1958. *The Letters of John Keats, 1814–1821*, 2 vols, ed. H. E. Rollins. Cambridge, Mass., Harvard University Press

Keats, J. 1978. *The Poems of John Keats*, ed. J. Stillinger. London,

Heinemann.

Larkin, P. 1988. *Collected Poems*, ed. A. Thwaite. London, The Marvell Press and Faber & Faber

Lodge, D. 1989. *Nice Work*. London, Penguin

MacLeish, A. 1952. *Collected Poems, 1917–1952*. Boston, Houghton Mifflin.

Proulx, A. 8 May 2004. 'Only the Lonely' in *The Guardian*

Proulx, A. 2006. *Close Range: Brokeback Mountain and other stories*. London: Harper Perennial

Proulx, A. 9 September 2008. Interview with R. J. Hughes, 'Return to the Range' in *The Wall Street Journal*. Consulted online at online.wsj.com/article/SB122065020058105139.html on 3 December 2008.

Roy, A. 1997. *The God of Small Things*. London, Flamingo

Rushdie, S. 1981. *Midnight's Children*. London, Cape

Shakespeare, W. 1974. *Henry IV, Part 1 and A Midsummer Night's Dream in The Riverside Shakespeare*. Boston: Houghton Mifflin

Sterne, L. 1998. *The Life and Opinions of Tristram Shandy, Gentleman*, ed. I. C. Ross. Oxford, Oxford University Press

Woolf, V. 2000. *To The Lighthouse*, ed. S. McNicholl. London, Penguin

Wordsworth, W. *The Lyrical Ballads*. 1991, ed. R. L. Brett & A. R. Jones. London, Routledge

# Bibliography of Critical and Theoretical Works

Allen, G., ed. 2006. *The Pupils of the University*. Special edition of *Parallax*, 40, July–September

Althusser, L. 1977. 'Ideology and Ideological State Apparatuses' and 'A Letter on Art', in *Lenin and Philosophy and Other Essays,* trans. Ben Brewster. London, New Left Books

Ashcroft, B. et al. 1998. *Key Concepts in Post-colonial Studies*. London, Routledge

Attridge, D. 2004. *The Singularity of Literature*. London, Routledge

Barthes, R. 1977. 'The Death of the Author', in *Image Music Text*, trans. S. Heath. London, Fontana

——1990. *S/Z*, trans. Richard Miller. Oxford, Basil Blackwell

Beauvoir, S. de 1972. *The Second Sex*, trans. H. M. Parshley. Harmondsworth, Penguin

Bhabha, H. 1994. *The Location of Culture*. London, Routledge

Birchall, C. 2006. *Knowledge Goes Pop: From Conspiracy Theory to Gossip*. London, Berg

Boumelha, P. 1999. 'The Patriarchy of Class', in *The Cambridge Companion to Thomas Hardy*, ed. D. Kramer. Cambridge, Cambridge University Press

Bowen, E. *The Mulberry Tree: Writings of Elizabeth Bowen*, ed. H. Lee. London, Vintage

Bridges, R. 1918. 'Preface to Notes' in *Poems of Gerard Manley Hopkins*. Oxford, Oxford University Press

Brooks, C. 1947. *The Well-Wrought Urn: Studies in the Structure of Poetry*. New York, Harcourt Brace

Brooks, P. 1984. *Reading for the Plot: Design and Intention in Narrative*. Oxford, Clarendon Press

Butler, J. 1990. *Gender Trouble: Feminism and the Subversion of Identity*. New York and London, Routledge

Chrisman, L. 1990. 'The Imperial Unconscious?: representations of imperial discourse', in *Critical Quarterly*, 32, 3

Cixous, H. 1999. 'Post-word', trans. E. Prenowitz in *Post Theory: New Directions in Criticism* ed. M. McQuillan, et al., Edinburgh, Edinburgh University Press.

——2000. 'Sorties', trans. Ann Liddle in *Modern Criticism and Theory: A Reader*, 2nd edn, eds D. Lodge and N. Wood. Harlow, Longman

——2009. *So Close*, trans. P. Kamuf. Cambridge, Polity

Clark, T. 2002. 'Literary Force, institutional values'. In Beaumont Bissell, E. *The Question of Literature: The Place of the Literary in Contemporary Theory*. Manchester, Manchester University Press

——2005. *The Poetics of Singularity: The Counter-Culturalist Turn in Heidegger, Derrida, Blanchot and the Later Gadamer.* Edinburgh, Edinburgh University Press

——2009. 'Call for Papers' for *Oxford Literary Review.* 31.1, (forthcoming 2010). Consulted online at http://www.eupjournals.com/action/showStoryContent?doi=10.3366%2F%2Fnews.2009.04.16.61 on 06.06.09.

Cornillon, S. K. ed. 1972. *Images of Women in Fiction: Feminist Perspectives.* Bowling Green, Ohio, Bowling Green University Popular Press

Culler, J. 1987. 'Criticism and Institutions: The American University' in *Poststructuralism and the Question of History,* D. Attridge et al ed. Cambridge, Cambridge University Press.

De Man, P. 1979. *Allegories of Reading Figural Language in Rousseau, Nietzsche, Rilke, and Proust.* New Haven and London, Yale University Press

——1986. *The Resistance to Theory.* Minneapolis, University of Minnesota Press.

——1989. *Blindness and Insight,* 2nd edn. London, Routledge

Derrida, J. 1982. *Margins of Philosophy,* trans. A. Bass. New York & London, Harvester Wheatsheaf

——1990. 'Some Statements and Truisms about Neologisms, Newisms, Postisms, Parasitisms, and Other Small Seismisms'. In *The States of "Theory",* ed. David Carroll. New York, Columbia University Press

——1992. '"This Strange Institution Called Literature": An Interview with Jacques Derrida', trans. G. Bennington and R. Bowlby in *Acts of Literature,* ed. D. Attridge. London, Routledge

——1997. *Of Grammatology,* trans. Gayatri Chakravorty Spivak. Baltimore, Johns Hopkins University Press

——2001. *Writing and Difference,* trans. A. Bass. Abingdon, Routledge

——2007. 'Final Words', trans. Gila Walker in *The Late Derrida,* eds. W. J. T. Mitchell and A. I. Davidson. Chicago, Chicago University Press

Eagleton, T. 1983. *Literary Theory: An Introduction*. Oxford, Blackwell

Elam, D. 2000. 'Deconstruction and Feminism' in *Deconstructions: A User's Guide*, ed. N. Royle. Basingstoke, Palgrave

Fish, S. 1980. *Is There a Text in this Class?: The Authority of Interpretive Communities*. Cambridge, MA, Harvard University Press

Forrester, J. 1997. *Dispatches from the Freud Wars: Psychoanalysis and Its Passions*. Cambridge, Mass, Harvard University Press

Foucault, M. 1980. 'Truth and Power' in *Power/Knowledge: Selected Interviews and Other Writings 1972–1977*, ed. C. Gordon. Hemel Hempstead, Harvester Wheatsheaf

Freud, S. 1953–1974. The Standard Edition of the Complete Psychological Works of Sigmund Freud, ed. James Strachey et al, 24 vols. London, Hogarth Press

——1995. *The Freud Reader*, ed. Peter Gay. London, Vintage

Friedan, B. 1963. *The Feminine Mystique*. New York, W. W. Norton

Friedman, S. S. 1989. 'Lyric Subversion of Narrative in Women's Writing: Virginia Woolf and the Tyranny of Plot' in *Reading Narrative: Form, Ethics, Ideology,* ed. J. Phelan. Columbus, Ohio State University Press

Gadamer, H-G. 1994. *Truth and Method* trans. J. Weinsheimer and D. G. Marshall. New York, Continuum

Genette, G. 1980. *Narrative Discourse: An Essay in Method*, trans. J. E. Lewin. Oxford, Basil Blackwell

Gilbert, S. and S. Gubar. 2000. *The Madwoman in the Attic: The Woman Writer and Nineteenth-Century Literary Imagination*, 2nd edn. New Haven and London, Yale University Press

Greenblatt, S. 1988. *'Invisible Bullets'* in *Shakespearean Negotiations: The Circulation of Social Energy in Renaissance England*. Oxford, Clarendon Press

Greer, G. 1970. *The Female Eunuch*. London, MacGibbon & Kee

Hillis Miller, J. 1999. *Black Holes/J. Hillis Miller; or Boustrophedonic Reading*. Stanford, Stanford University Press

Holland, N. 1968. *The Dynamics of Literary Response*. Oxford, Oxford University Press

——1975. *Five Readers Reading*. London, Yale University Press.

Irigaray, L. 1985. *This Sex Which is Not One*, trans. C. Porter. New York, Cornell University Press

Iser, W. 1995. 'Interaction between Text and Reader', in *Readers and Reading*, ed. A. Bennett. London: Longman

Jackobson, R. 1987. 'What is Poetry' in *Language and Literature*, ed. K. Pomorska and R. Rudy Cambridge MA, Belknap Press of Harvard University Press

Kamuf, P. 1997. *The Division of Literature, or the University in Deconstruction*. Chicago, Chicago University Press

Knox, R. 1850. *The Races of man: A Fragment*. London, Renshaw

Lacan, J. 1977. *Écrits: A Selection*, trans. A. Sheridan. London, Tavistock

Laplanche, J. and J-B. Pontalis, 1983. *The Language of Psychoanalysis*, trans. Donald Nicholson-Smith. London, Hogarth Press

Leitsch, V, ed. 2001. *The Norton Anthology of Theory and Criticism*. New York and London, Norton

Lennard, J. 1996. *The Poetry Handbook: A Guide to Reading Poetry for Pleasure and Practical Criticism*. Oxford, Oxford University Press

Louth, C. 1998. *Hölderlin and the Dynamics of Translation*. Oxford, Legenda

Lukács, G. 1963. *The Meaning of Contemporary Realism*, trans. J. and N. Mander. London: Merlin

——1970. 'Art and Objective Truth' in *Writer, Critic and Other Essays*, ed. A. Kahn. London, Merlin

McClintock, A. 1992. 'The Angel of Progress' in *Social Text*, 31/32, 84–97

McEwan, N. 2000. *Hard Times: York Notes Advanced*. Harlow, Longman

Macksey, R. and E. Donato, eds. 1972. *The Structuralist Controversy: The Languages of Criticism and the Science of Man*. Baltimore and London, The Johns Hopkins University Press

Marx, K. 1976. *Marx, Engels on Literature and Art*. Moscow, Progress Publishers

——1977 *Karl Marx: Selected Writings*, ed. D McLellan. Oxford, Oxford University Press

Marxist-Feminist Literature Collective. 1978. 'Women's writing: *Jane Eyre, Shirley, Villette, Aurora Leigh*', in *Ideology and Consciousness*, 1, 3, Spring, 27–48

Mill, J. S. 1984. 'The Subjection of Women', in *Collected Works*, vol. 21, ed. J. M. Robson, Toronto, University of Toronto Press, 1984

Najder, Z. 2007. *Joseph Conrad: A Life*. Rochester, NY, Camden House

Ngugi wa Thiong'o. 1986. *Decolonizing the Mind: The Politics of Language in African Culture*. London, Heinemann

Nietzsche, F. 1959. *The Genealogy of Morals & Ecce Homo*, trans. W. Kaufmann and R. J. Hollingdale. New York, Vintage Books

——1974. *The Gay Science, with a Prelude in Rhymes and an Appendix of Songs*, trans. W. Kaufmann. New York, Vintage Books, 1974

——1989. 'On Truth and Lying in an Extra-moral Sense' in *Friedrich Nietzsche on Rhetoric and Language*, ed. and trans. S L. Gilman et al. Oxford, Oxford University Press

Okara, G. 1963. 'African Speech ... English Words' in *Transition,* 10, 15–16

Puttenham, G. 1968. *The Arte of English Poesie, 1589*. Menston, Scolar Press

Readings, B. 1994. *The University in Ruins*. Cambridge MA, Harvard University Press

Rivkin, J. and M. Ryan. 2004. *Literary Theory: An Anthology*. Oxford, Blackwell

Royle, N. 1991. *Literature and Telepathy*. Oxford, Blackwell

Said, E. 1993. *Culture and Imperialism*. London, Chatto and Windus

——1995. *Orientalism*, 2nd edn. London, Penguin

Saussure, F. 1983. *Course in General Linguistics*, trans. R. Harris. London, Duckworth

Selden, R., ed. 1988. *The Theory of Criticism from Plato to the Present: A Reader*. London and New York, Longman

Shklovsky, V. 1965. 'Art as Technique', in *Russian Formalist Criticism: Four Essays*, eds L. T. Lemon and Marion J. Reis. Lincoln, University of Nebraska Press

Showalter, E. 1977. *A Literature of Their Own: British Women Novelists from Brontë to Lessing*. Princeton, NJ, Princeton University Press

Showalter, E. 1981. 'Feminist Criticism in the Wilderness' in *Critical Inquiry* 8, 179–205

Smith, C. H. 1848. *The Natural History of the Human Species*. Edinburgh

Stape, J. 2006. *The Several Lives of Joseph Conrad*. London, Heinemann

Todorov, T. 1977. *The Poetics of Prose*, trans. R. Howard. Oxford, Basil Blackwell

Veeser, H. A. 1994. *The New Historicism Reader*. New York, Routledge

Watts, C. 1977. 'The mirror-tale: an ethico-structural analysis of Conrad's "The Secret Sharer" ' in *Critical Quarterly,* 19.3

Wimsatt, W. K. 1954. *The Verbal Icon: Studies in the Meaning of Poetry*. Kentucky, University of Kentucky Press

——1965. *Hateful Contraries: Studies in Literature and Criticism*. Lexington, University of Kentucky Press

Wood, S. 2004. 'Try Thinking as If Perhaps ...' in *Études britanniques contemporaines* 25, 159–79

Young, R. 1995. *Colonial Desire: Hybridity in Culture, Theory and Race*. London and New York, Routledge

# Index

# A Beginner's Guide to Existentialism

**Existentialism**
Thomas E. Wartenberg

978-1-85168-593-6
£9.99 / $14.95

In this lively and topical introduction, Wartenberg reveals a vibrant mode of philosophical inquiry that addresses concerns at the heart of the existence of every human being. Wartenberg uses classic films, novels, and plays to present the ideas of thinkers from Nietzsche and Camus to Sartre and Heidegger.

"Thomas Wartenberg's engaging book will make existentialism come alive for a new generation of readers. It clarifies key existentialist concepts and helps us all appreciate why existentialism was philosophy's most exciting contribution to twentieth-century thought."
**Gareth B. Matthews** – author and Professor of Philosophy at the University of Massachusetts, Amherst

"It addresses the student in terms that make sense in their lives." **Arthur C. Danto** – author, art critic, and Johnsonian Professor Emeritus of Philosophy at Columbia University

**THOMAS E. WARTENBERG** is Professor of Philosophy at Mount Holyoke College, Massachusetts, USA. He is the author of *Unlikely Couples: Movie Romance as Social Criticism*.

# A Beginner's Guide to Humanism

Showing how humanists make sense of the world using reason, experience, and sensitivity, Cave emphasizes that we can, and should, flourish without God. Lively, provocative, and refreshingly rant-free, this book is essential reading for all — whether atheist, agnostic, believer, or of no view — who wish better to understand what it means to be human.

978-1-85168-644-5
£9.99 / $14.95

"An admirable guide for all those non-religious who may wake up to the fact that they are humanists." **Sir Bernard Crick** – Emeritus Professor of Birkbeck College, University of London, and author of *Democracy: A Very Short Introduction*

"Humanism is loving, sharing and caring and above all an intelligent philosophical way to make the best of our own and our neighbours' lives. I could not commend it more." **Clare Rayner** – Broadcaster, writer and Vice President of the British Humanist Association

Writer and broadcaster Peter Cave teaches philosophy for The Open University and City University London. Author of the bestselling *Can A Robot Be Human?*, he chairs the Humanist Philosophers' Group, frequently contributes to philosophy journals and magazines, and has presented several philosophy programmes for the BBC. He lives in London.

Browse further titles at
www.oneworld-publications.com

# A Beginner's Guide to Feminism

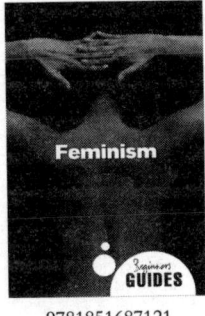

9781851687121
£9.99/ $14.95

By highlighting the themes that form the enduring nexuses between its various strands, taking powerful examples from feminist campaigns, and tackling timely issues such as genocide and war rape, Scholtz invites us to join in with the lively debates and always germane challenges of feminism.

"This book is written so clearly, cogently, and cleverly that anyone who reads it carefully will be persuaded that all societies should become more feminist." **Rosemarie Tong** – Distinguished Professor in Health Care Ethics, University of North Carolina at Charlotte

"Cleverly combines a broad range of topics with careful scholarship, all laid out in friendly and accessible prose." **Hilde Lindemann** – Professor of Philosophy, Michigan State University.

**SALLY J. SCHOLZ** is is Professor of Philosophy at Villanova University, Pennsylvania, and faculty-in-residence at its Center for Peace and Justice Studies.

Browse further titles at
www.oneworld-publications.com

# A Beginner's Guide to Psychology

From TV experts to the amateur musings of your best friend, the language of psychology has permeated all aspects of every-day life. This Beginner's Guide is informed by the latest cutting-edge research and provides a vibrant and witty examination of the very heart of what it is to be human.

### Psychology
G. Neil Martin

978-1-85168-578-3
£9.99 /$14.95

Can personality and intelligence be measured?

Is being physically attractive an advantage?

Is it really better to forgive and forget?

How do babies learn to perceive and think?

Can listening to Mozart improve IQ?

What happens when we sleep?

**DR G. NEIL MARTIN** is Reader in Psychology, a Fellow of the RSA, a Chartered Scientist, and Director of the Human Olfaction Laboratory at Middlesex University, UK. He has written several books on psychology and neuroscience, and co-authored the first online course in introductory psychology in Europe.

Browse further titles at
www.oneworld-publications.com

# A Beginner's Guide to Philosophy of Mind

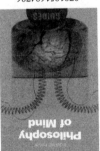

In this lively and entertaining introduction to the philosophy of mind, Edward Feser explores the questions central to the discipline, such as 'do computers think?', and 'what is consciousness?'; and gives an account of all the most important and significant attempts that have been made to answer them.

9781851684786
£9.99 / $14.95

"A splendid, highly accessible and lucid introduction. The arguments are engaging and provide a refreshing challenge to some of the conventional assumptions in the field."

**Charles Taliaferro** – Professor of Philosophy, St Olaf College, Minnesota

"Feser has a feel for the enduring problems…an excellent introduction."

**John Haldane** – Professor of Philosophy, University of St Andrews

**EDWARD FESER** is Visiting Assistant Professor of Philosophy at Loyola Marymount University, California, and the author of On Nozick. He has taught and written widely in the areas of philosophy of mind, and his most recent research has focused on new solutions to the mind/body problem

Browse further titles at
www.oneworld-publications.com

# A Beginner's Guide to Philosophy of Religion

Assuming no prior knowledge of philosophy from the reader, Taliaferro provides a clear exploration of the discipline, introducing a wide range of philosophers and covering the topics of morality and religion, evil, the afterlife, prayer, and miracles.

9781851686506

£9.99/ $14.95

"Brimming with arguments, the material is cutting edge, and the selection of topics is superb."
**J.P. Moreland** – Professor of Philosophy, St Olaf College, Minnesota

"Covers all the most important issues in a way that is always fair-minded, and manages to be accessible without over-simplifying." **John Cottingham** – President of the British Society for the Philosophy of Religion and Professor Emeritus of Philosophy, Reading University

**CHARLES TALIAFERRO** is Professor of Philosophy at St. Olaf College, Minnesota, USA. He is the author or editor of numerous books on the philosophy of religion including as co-editor of *The Blackwell Companion to Philosophy of Religion*.

Browse further titles at
www.oneworld-publications.com